Mayor Nicola Smith
Grateful Steward

by Patricia Vaccarino

North Star Publishing

North Star Publishing • Seattle

Mayor Nicola Smith *Grateful Steward*
By Patricia Vaccarino

This book first published in 2021 by North Star Publishing

ISBN: 978-1-7379944-1-1

Cover design by Josue Mora
Original cover photo of Mayor Nicola Smith by Magic Photo, Lynnwood, WA
Formal Portrait of Nicola and Del Smith and Family by Chad Bridwell
All other photos provided courtesy of Mayor Nicola Smith

Library of Congress Control Number: 2021920040
Printed in the U.S.

Table of Contents

Acknowledgments

"This book has been made possible because of the friendship, support and professionalism of Patricia Vaccarino. I also want to thank Julie Moore for her selfless contribution of time and expertise in fact-checking and photo selections. My deepest gratitude for bringing my vision to reality and leaving an accurate legacy for the people." – **Mayor Nicola Smith**

Dedication

"With heartfelt devotion and gratitude to my family, my husband, Del, daughters Emily and Tia, and especially to my four grandchildren, Julian Angel, Kendall Kay, Skylar Penelope and Elijah Theos. I want my grandchildren to know that my journey as mayor was "Kinda a Big Deal" and I want to inspire them to be gracious leaders wherever life takes them. As we journey through life, we are all 'Better Together.' Thank you to everyone who participated in this story and for your commitment to being the best you can be." -**Mayor Nicola Smith**

Native American Prayer Page

"Please join us in respectfully acknowledging that the City of Lynnwood is on the traditional lands of the Coast Salish people. Join us in a moment of reflection and respect to acknowledge and recognize that indigenous people have lived in North America since time immemorial and honor the contributions of those both past and present who have shaped our current lives."

Preface

We live during a time in history when we might have lost touch with the core values of what makes an effective leader. Then, when someone comes along who is the epitome of true leadership, we feel a sense of relief. It is reassuring to know that there are elected officials who have integrity. One such person is Mayor Nicola Smith.

From 2014 to 2021, Nicola Smith served as the seventh mayor of Lynnwood, Washington, a small city located in Snohomish County. She has been described by many as a mayor with a heart. If you ask her about her leadership style and why she has been able to get so much done for her city in such a short time, she describes herself as a *servant-leader*.

Being the mayor of a city is not an easy job. Doing the job well requires untold hours of service, dedication, sacrifice and more. Focus. Determination. Keeping an eye on the ball. Showing courage in the face of adversity. Listening well. Keeping one's ear to the ground. Being open to the people. Having the wisdom, the heart and the passion to serve.

Being an elected official is derived from the heart of our democracy—Of the people, by the people, for the people, but ultimately being a good leader is about taking care of the people. Being a good leader is being a good steward. Mayor Nicola Smith left her city in a better state than she found it. We can all take a lesson in stewardship from her. Stewardship affects every aspect of our lives, from how well we take care of our homes, our work and our families to how well we take care of our communities.

Here is a story about a remarkable woman who was destined to be the mayor of Lynnwood, Washington. Her story needs to be told beyond the borders of a small but growing city in the state of Washington. Her story embodies those qualities that we all need to look for when we elect our leaders. Mayor Nicola Smith is an inspiration to young people. She is an inspiration to us all. This is what true leadership looks like.

- **Patricia Vaccarino**

Chapter 1
What is a Mayor?

When Nicola Smith appeared on the political scene in 2013, her candidacy to become mayor of Lynnwood, Washington seemed to be a spur-of-the-moment decision. New to politics, she had never run for office or served on the Lynnwood City Council. Nor had she ever received any sort of political appointment. For 27 years, Nicola Smith had spent the bulk of her career moving up through the ranks at Edmonds College (known previously as Edmonds Community College), where she held a succession of administrative positions. Everyone who knew her at the college remarked on her ability to hire good people, nurture those people, organize teams, collaborate and get the job done. Her leadership skills were uncontested. Certainly, she had excellent communication skills and was a whiz at organizational management. More than anything, she was known to be a good listener.

Nicola, as she was called back then and is still called by everyone, family, friends, business associates and colleagues alike, did have an uncanny ability to listen well. She had a reputation for listening to the people around her and always responding in a positive way. She was also known to never shy away from having difficult conversations. Theoretically, all of these skills would transfer well from Edmonds College to Lynnwood City Hall. The reality of entering the political realm, however, soon became an eye-opening experience. After enduring a hotly debated and contentious campaign, she learned the gravitas of exactly what it means to be a mayor.

Prior to winning the election by a wide margin against incumbent Mayor Don Gough, Nicola had already planned a Rotary volunteer service project that would take her to Haiti. "I knew I had been elected mayor," she said, "but it was also important to follow through on the trip." The project entailed visiting a combined health facility and school complex, where the volunteer team was slated to renovate a water system so the children would have clean water for drinking, cooking and bathing. The volunteer team, including Nicola's husband Del and her twenty-year-old daughter Tia, would also work on the facility's bathroom and kitchen and bring along medical supplies for the children. It would be weeks before Nicola would be sworn in as mayor, so she never anticipated the slightest protest from anyone.

When city staff member **Frantz Jocelyn Donat** learned of her trip to Haiti, he became very upset that his new mayor would be going to such a dangerous place. Wrought with emotion, he protested, saying, "You can't go, you can't do this!" Frantz was very upset that his new mayor was going to go to this country without protection. He knew firsthand of the civil unrest and potential danger that could lie ahead for Mayor-elect Nicola Smith. Haiti was Frantz Donat's homeland. Although he had been in the United States for twenty-three years, he still had deep roots in Haiti and connections he could call upon to help if needed. What happened next demonstrated how important a mayor is to the people. Frantz Donat's work required him to do a little bit of everything for the City of Lynnwood. Mainly he worked as a records and procurement tech, but the measures he took to protect his mayor from harm went far beyond the scope of his job with the city. When he realized he could not stop Nicola from following through on her service commitment, he took matters into his own hands. Unbeknownst to Mayor-elect Smith, Frantz Donat called in a few favors.

When Nicola arrived in Haiti, the airport was teeming with military police armed with machine guns. The entire volunteer team, including Nicola, was unaware that the military police had been sent there to protect her. From the airport, they rode on a school bus, where they visited a medical clinic and school compound in Plaine-du-Nord, north of the capital of Port-au-Prince. They built a new kitchen and new toilets at the compound, and they installed a water purification system that had the capacity to serve thousands of people. Nicola, along with her husband and daughter Tia, and other Rotary members and volunteers, slept on yoga mats on the concrete floor of the compound.

Gunnvor Tveidt was also part of the project team that had gone to Haiti. She remembers Frantz Donat as being very supportive when he learned the mayor-elect along with other Rotarians would be going to Haiti. "Everyone was concerned about Nicola's safety," Gunnvor Tveidt recalled. "When we arrived, there were guards everywhere. We thought it was normal. We did not know that through Frantz the military was there to guard Nicola."

The police stayed close on Nicola's heels, following her around the compound and everywhere she went. Every move she made was closely guarded; every restaurant she went to, every person she spoke to, was duly noted and reported to Frantz Donat, who was operating his own self-styled, rogue security headquarters back home in Lynnwood.

Frantz says, "I knew Haiti was going through political turmoil and my brother happened to be in the Dominican Republic and I asked him to give her some protection. He flew to Haiti and offered his protection. He had people watching over her, but she didn't know. Haiti was not a good place to be at that time—that was 2013. My brother had connections with the chief of police in Haiti. The police had detectives following her wherever she went in Haiti."

After Nicola returned to the United States, one day she and Frantz were having a conversation. Before she had a chance to tell him where she had been in Haiti, he knew the details about everywhere she had been. Nicola knew that had to be more than a coincidence. Until then she had not known that she was being followed and protected. Frantz Donat had done everything possible to protect his mayor.

To Frantz Donat's way of thinking, the mayor plays a central role in every society. If you look at the history of the United States, Americans were building small cities like Lynnwood from the beginning. "Everything started in small cities—they are the bones of this country," he said. "Every mayor plays a key role in the city all over the United States. Because mayors love their country, and they are loyal to their city, they can get the citizens to vote. Anywhere in the world, the mayor plays a key role for citizens."

If you live in a city anywhere in the world, chances are you have been directly impacted by your mayor. The actual term *Mayor* has its linguistic roots in the military rank of Major, ultimately derived from the French *Majeur*. Worldwide, the mayor is the highest ranking official in a municipal government. While mayors hail from the far corners of the globe, regardless of their local customs or cultures, the scope of their work is universal.

Mayors everywhere are responsible for their city's day-to-day administration. Mayors preside over council meetings, and work with their local legislature to create and enact law. Mayors make multitudes of business decisions every day. Some decisions are as small as choosing the color palette of a wrap for trash cans. Other decisions are as large-scale and as awe-inspiring as negotiating federal funding for new mass transportation infrastructure: connecting trains, buses, major arterials, waterways, bridges and roads. Because mayors are constantly making so many decisions that affect the well-being of their city, they must get accurate and timely information from their constituents and stakeholders. Ensuring that their decisions are informed and smart, mayors are saddled with the responsibility of keeping their ear to the ground to listen to all of the people in their community.

The mayor is closer to the people than any other elected public official. Yet, unless a city's citizens have the opportunity to witness a mayor in action on a daily basis, most don't have any idea of what it takes to do the job. A mayor's actions, large and small, have a long-lasting impact on the people: how a city is run; what gets built and what does not get built; how the city looks aesthetically; and how a city is kept safe—free from crime, fire, damage, destruction of property, loss and theft; how the city manages major health crisis like a global pandemic; how much the city's residents pay in tax; how a city takes care of its citizens; how a city welcomes newcomers and sets the tone for its culture and customs, all of these decisions fall within the domain of the mayor. From ribbon-cutting events to commemorate the opening of a new store or park to the formal ceremonies welcoming sports teams or sister city delegations, there you will find your mayor.

There are approximately 20,000 municipal governments in the United States. Many small towns use the council-manager system and have a *weak* mayor-council system of governance. Almost all large cities in the United States have *Strong* Mayor systems. Towns with small populations, usually 5,000 or less, are not incorporated and are overseen by the county government.

Much has been written about the two types of mayoral governance: Strong mayor versus weak mayor. Under the *Strong Mayor* model, the mayor is elected by the people in a general election, whereas in the *Weak Mayor* model, the mayor is appointed by the city council. The weak mayor functions as a rubber-stamp official who shows up at public ceremonies, often acting as the face of the city, but in reality, the weak mayor does not really run the city—that job is left to the city manager or an equivalent municipal administrator.

Most cities in America, including Lynnwood, Washington, favor the strong mayor model—these strong mayors are elected by the people that they serve and act as a centralized executive authority or the CEO of the city. The mayor directs the city's administrative departments and has the power to hire and fire department heads. While the city council has the power to make and enact laws, the council does not manage the city's overall daily operations. The mayor has veto power, and, in most cases, can cast a tie-breaking vote. Also, when it is necessary, a strong mayor can exert mayoral leadership through the binding authority of *Executive Action*.

A mayor can exercise leadership over her constituency for good or ill-gotten gains. A mayor's inactivity, neglect or incompetence can also irreparably damage a city. Mayors have earned the reputation of being showmen, clowns or even bullies. For better or for worse, throughout American history, there have been legendary mayors. Mayor Richard Daley of Chicago, oft-described as "the last of the Big City bosses," has the distinction of being the mayor who served the longest—for twenty-two years. New York City produced the reputedly "best" mayor, Fiorello La Guardia. Another Chicago Mayor, William H. "Big Bill" Thompson, set the record for being the most overtly corrupt after having accepted campaign funds from notorious gangsters, including Al Capone.

Only one mayor went on to achieve the height of political ambition—Buffalo Mayor Grover Cleveland became the 22nd and 24th President of the United States. He is also the only U.S. President to have served two nonconsecutive terms. Not all notable mayors preside over large cities. Pete Buttigieg, mayor of South Bend, Indiana, ran for President in 2020. A graduate of Harvard, a Rhodes Scholar and a Navy Reserve Lieutenant, Buttigieg has the distinction of being the first openly gay presidential candidate.

Some mayors come to the office because they feel called to fix what is broken. Aja Brown returned to her hometown of Compton, California in 2013 to serve as the city's youngest mayor. She was a woman with a deeply personal mission. In the 1970s, Aja Brown's grandmother was murdered in Compton. Aja Brown's plan as mayor was to give Compton a makeover. Since then, unemployment and gang violence have taken a back seat to the city's growing economic revitalization that includes attracting large businesses like UPS.

There are thousands of mayors in the United States alone. The United States Conference of Mayors is the official non-partisan organization of cities with a population of 30,000 or larger. Each city is represented by its chief elected official, the mayor. The organization comprises over 1,400 mayors from across the United States. The job of being mayor is much harder than most jobs. While becoming a mayor might seem to be a good political opportunity, it is fraught with challenges that would crush an ordinary individual. The untold hours spent providing leadership over a city requires enormous sacrifice, a commitment of time, energy and devotion. If you want to know who is kept up at night worrying about the state of your city, you will find your mayor.

Politicians aspire to be mayor for any number of reasons: a strong desire to serve the public, to attain power and visibility on a local stage, to obtain a steppingstone for higher political ambitions, or to do a good job, one they believe only they can do. These are only a few reasons. Our story here is about a woman who did not have political ambitions and had never thought of running for public office. Nicola Smith did not seek to become mayor of Lynnwood, Washington. Instead, Nicola Smith was asked to run for mayor, not once, but repeatedly. A wide range of citizens thought Nicola Smith was the right person at the right time who could steer the City of Lynnwood in a new direction. Haitian immigrant Frantz Jocelyn Donat thought so highly of Nicola Smith that he found a way to protect her before she had even been sworn in as mayor. The story of Mayor Nicola Smith is also the story of many people in the Lynnwood community who thought their city was destined to be a star among cities, the north star.

Chapter 2
All Roads Lead to Lynnwood

Lynnwood is a small city in Snohomish County that is located 16 miles north of Seattle, 13 miles south of Everett, and 15 miles from Bellevue. Lynnwood bears the cartographic distinction of being situated on the nexus of two Interstate freeways, Interstate 5 (I-5) running north-south, and Interstate 405 (I-405), connecting Lynnwood to the Bellevue-Redmond area; and two additional state highways: State Route 99, running north to Everett and south to Seattle, and State Route 524, connecting to the city of Edmonds in the west via 196th Street Southwest. Lynnwood's close proximity to Edmonds makes it easily accessible to the major waterway of the Puget Sound and public ferry service. To suggest that Lynnwood is a busy place from a transportation perspective is an understatement. Akin to the brilliant aqueduct system of ancient Rome, all roads in the Pacific Northwest eventually lead to Lynnwood.

The Lynnwood of today originally sprung up on the traditional lands of the Coast Salish people. Indigenous people inhabited the area long before the area was logged and settled by homesteaders in the 19th and 20th Centuries. Later the Snohomish tribe used the area for hunting, fishing and agricultural activities. The Snohomish relocated to the Tulalip reservation after the signing of the Treaty of Point Elliot in 1855.

Named *Lynnwood* for the wife of Seattle realtor **Karl O'Brien** in the 1940s, the area became known for the development of Alderwood Manor, a planned farming community. It has been often stated, somewhat ruefully that Lynnwood started out as a bunch of people trying to get out of the city and into the country to start chicken farms. Lynnwood was incorporated on April 23, 1959, and began spreading in a slow suburban sprawl. By 1977, the opening of the mega shopping mall *Alderwood* transformed the area inhabited by creeping chicken farms into a popular retail and office district. Anchored by the Alderwood Mall, Lynnwood grew to have one of the largest number of retailers and businesses in the Puget Sound region, and yet it never had a downtown city center.

In the 2010 U.S. Census, the population was reported to be 35,836. Even without having access to 2020 census data, the city's population is estimated to have increased by nearly 10%, but the real explosion of growth is yet to come. A major factor for this anticipated growth is due to the expansion of the light rail that is currently under construction and slated to begin operation in Lynnwood in 2024.

Sound Transit's light rail Rapid Transit System has been serving the Seattle Metropolitan area since 2009. Clean, efficient and quiet, the Link Light Rail system is state-of-the-art transportation that now runs fully on carbon emissions-free renewable energy. Initially, the light rail ran from downtown Seattle to Tukwila, but by December 2009 the system was extended to Seattle-Tacoma (SeaTac) International Airport. Other expansions were quickly planned around the Puget Sound region. In fact, Sound Transit's ballot measure in 2008, known as Sound Transit 2, approved several light rail extensions that included service to Lynnwood. According to Sound Transit CEO **Peter Rogoff**, "The introduction of the light rail is going to have a dramatic and meaningful impact on Lynnwood."

Sound Transit's Link Light Rail to Lynnwood is indeed a major catalyst to the growth of the city, but it's also important to note that for years key stakeholders and businesspeople in the Lynnwood community were intent on creating a downtown core for Lynnwood. **Jean Hales,** past President and CEO of the South Snohomish Chamber of Commerce, spoke of the plans that were made for Lynnwood long before the light rail was on anyone's radar. As far back as 2001, a group of developers had partnered with the city to completely revitalize Lynnwood and to create a city center. "A heart for the community was so needed," Hales said.

Despite the detailed development plan that had been created for the downtown city center, nothing had been done for years. When asked why the development plans never went anywhere, Jean Hales stated the reasons based on her observations: "The lack of sophistication among the Lynnwood City Council, staffing issues, the wrong people were in place in the wrong jobs. A handful of excellent staff members were completely stifled because of the poor leadership. No progress could be made. It was seriously upside-down," she said.

Both within the Lynnwood business community and to businesspeople outside of the community, the City of Lynnwood had a reputation for being difficult. **Kevin McKay**, the former VP for finance and operations at Edmonds College, remembered "On average we were seeing about $80,000 being added to each of our projects. Inspection at the end of a project always found something wrong, a lot of change orders and a lot of cost was added to each project." McKay also recalls the morale of city hall as being low. "Architects and contractors actually refused to bid on some college projects because of the reputation of Lynnwood's planning/inspection departments for causing delays and adding costs to projects."

According to the city Public Affairs Officer **Julie Moore**, "In 2013, we were all just trying to survive. Departments worked in silos and there was a lack of cohesive leadership. We lost employees to layoffs, and some talented employees left for better opportunities – the staff left was overburdened and underresourced. There was conflict everywhere, from the Mayor's Office to Council and even amongst department heads."

The simple process of applying for a business license required four separate filings in four departments, all located in different buildings. The four departments, Community Development, Economic Development, Public Works and the Fire Marshal, operated in silos. The four departments didn't talk to one another, didn't work with one another, and did not do a whole lot to be helpful. Some businesspeople have asserted that, at the time, some city staff members did everything they could do to impede progress. The whole application process was complicated and not easily accessible to businesses. There was so much red tape, and it was totally unnecessary. The four departments also had a high turnover of staff.

Business owner **Phong Nguyen** graduated from the University of Washington and became a computer engineer in Silicon Valley. Phong and his mother Anna (Anh Vu) had come to the United States as a refugee on a boat from Vietnam in 1979. She worked three jobs before opening Anna's Home Furnishings with her husband, who was Phong's stepfather. Their business had three locations, all in Lynnwood for 26 years. Phong's mother asked her son to come back to Seattle to help run the family business when his stepfather's health declined.

Phong Nguyen remembers his experience of dealing with the city to replace a dilapidated storage unit behind his business with a simple garbage shed.

"Before I came back, we had a storage shed behind our building that we used to put our recycled garbage into. It had been there for at least 10 years. It was looking really dilapidated and homeless people started sleeping in it. I called my buddy, a roommate in college, who was a contractor. He helped me put up new siding on my garbage shed. We worked two weekends on that project. We wanted to model the look of the Lynnwood Convention Center. He designed it and worked it out. We used all of the existing structure and put an aluminum roof and siding on it. We were 90% of the way done, just putting the doors on it, when a gentleman from the city walked into the business and said, '*I noticed you built a new shed.*' He said we needed to get a permit. I told him it was there for 15 years. He said, '*Anything you do in this city, you need to get a permit. You have to measure to get setbacks and get engineering plans.*' I asked him what setbacks are and he said, 'I don't know.'"

After the inspector left, Phong called the permitting office. He asked the clerk if he was required to get a permit just to re-side his storage shed. "We were just residing it with aluminum and the clerk I phoned said, 'oh no.' I told her what the inspector had said. She said, 'You will have to talk to him about it.'"

"They told me I needed to hire an architect, get a site plan, elevation drawings, and measure all of the setbacks. It was going to be a couple of hundred dollars for the permit but to hire an architect to do the plans... I didn't have a budget for that."

"The city didn't make it a user-friendly experience at that time."

If dealing with the city was like slogging through quicksand for small-business owners like Phong Nguyen, larger business owners also experienced unnecessary delays and outright stonewalling. Housing Developer **Jeffrey Butler** is behind the development of Triton Court. This new Residence Hall, located across the street from campus, finished construction in July and opened in September 2020. It is located right across the street from Rainier Place Residence Hall. Triton Court was designed for Edmonds College and Central Washington University students ages 16 and older who want to live in a community focused on student living.

According to Jeffrey Butler, "Lynnwood suffered from a Small-town Complex. The people I would submit my plans to... they had large personalities, larger than what their role entitled them to. My plans were directly from the IBC International Building Codes—those are state of Washington mandated codes, but the City of Lynnwood did not always abide by those codes."

Butler recalls his frustration when the city could not justify its reason for wanting to make changes to his plans. A developer is often taking a big risk, millions of dollars are on the line, yet a project could end up "sitting at the back of the desk for months."

Jean Hales remembers the city's permitting process had a culture that was anti-customer service. "Fraught with problems, delays and a bad attitude, it was the antithesis of customer service," she said. Some developers told her it was the worst permitting process that they had ever encountered. One developer who flew into Lynnwood, to seek potential properties and possibilities for projects, told Jean Hales: "You guys are sitting on a gold mine here, but we couldn't make any progress."

Businesswoman and mortgage professional **Tatyana Sineeva** remembers it was very difficult to get permits for construction. "The builders, contractors were complaining about it. At that time, we were in economic recovery after 2008, and it was really hard to project growth for the city. It was really difficult for the city to do any innovation. I was in touch with many businesspeople who said it was a very delayed and difficult process—that it was a barrier to people getting back up on their feet."

Educator, business owner and community volunteer, **Inae Piercy** recalls the problems Lynnwood faced back in 2013. There was a prevailing attitude that people did not want to live in Lynnwood. Instead, they wanted to have an Edmonds address. With the realization that the light rail was coming, people wanted to see the beautification of Lynnwood. There was a new consciousness evolving in which people were saying, "I want to live in Lynnwood."

As President and CEO of the South Snohomish Chamber of Commerce, Jean Hales knew firsthand of the concerns of the business community. Hales and others saw the potential for a downtown city center and knew it would be wonderful if only they could get the plan that had long ago been created, to move forward. The inevitability of the light rail hub coming created a new sense of urgency. At that juncture in 2013, Lynnwood was known for three things: its suburban sprawl, Alderwood Mall and an inept city bureaucracy. None of the elements were in place to manage the change that was needed for business, housing, health and Public Safety, roads, transportation and the well-being of the city's citizens. Lynnwood wasn't going anywhere. The city was in a bad place and stuck.

George Smith, (no relation to Nicola Smith), who was vice president of student services at Edmonds College, identified why the City of Lynnwood wasn't moving forward in 2013. "The city government was disjointed politically," he said. "There was a lot of animosity on the city council and animosity between the mayor and the council members. There was a void in leadership."

When George Smith first moved to Lynnwood from Kirkland in 1991, "There was a strong mayor," he said. "Mayor Meryl Hrdlicka." Smith was asked by Mayor Hrdlicka, known as "Herk," to serve on the planning commission. "It was a real learning experience for me to become involved in city politics. It was interesting to follow a few of the council members as they were elected to the mayor position, but in my opinion, they had a difficult time because of the divisiveness and political discord."

Rev. M. Christopher Boyer is the pastor at Good Shepherd Baptist Church, but he also served on the Lynnwood City Council From 2013 to the end of 2017. He remembers the state of the City of Lynnwood in 2013. "When talking about city government there was a real sense of fear, of employees being disempowered and looking over their shoulders to see who would next get fired. The city had not recovered from the 2008 recession. There was not a lot of excitement about the direction of the city government. We knew light rail would come, but there was no way the city could take advantage of these opportunities."

2013 was a mayoral election year. Jean Hales had a deep understanding that if Lynnwood was going to move forward in a positive direction, then the city needed to have the right kind of leadership—a good mayor. She put together a list of qualifications: someone who had administrative ability; someone who knew how to listen; someone who was a quick study, and above all the mayor needed to be articulate and have integrity. Then she created a list of names of people to interview. The filing date to run for mayor was May 2013 and quickly approaching. Hales, who knew Nicola Smith from the Lynnwood Rotary Club, was certain that not only did Nicola have all of the qualifications, but she was also strong in all areas.

Another person who knew Nicola Smith through Rotary was **Judge Jeffrey D. Goodwin**, a district court judge for Snohomish County South Division in Snohomish County, Washington. He remembers meeting Nicola long before she was asked to run for mayor. At the time she was with Edmonds College. Judge Goodwin stated, "One of the things I admired about her is a real desire for service and empathy. When people start Rotary, it is because they want to make business contacts and that's fine, but Rotary is so much more than that—a passion for service and a strong desire to do good things in their community."

Businesswoman and mortgage professional **Tatyana Sineeva,** who also served on the Rotary Club with Nicola Smith, commented how Nicola was always very approachable and brought people together. "She is open, smart and always makes the best of the situation."

"For Nicola, those attitudes (the real desire for service and an empathy) really come from her core." Judge Goodwin added. "To take on this thankless job of government leadership takes a lot of courage, empathy and patience, and an ability to communicate."

One evening Jean Hales called Nicola at home in the evening. Hales recalls saying to Nicola, "I have something I want to talk to you about, but I want you to pour a glass of wine first and sit down. You can tell me to go to hell if you want... ."

Nicola had not given much thought to becoming mayor until Jean Hales asked her to run for office. For years, Hales had been more than a colleague and a community leader, she was also a trusted friend. The discussion with Hales made her realize that the role of a mayor was a managerial job, and that's exactly what she had done in higher education, but would that suffice among naysayers from the incumbent mayor's team and the people of Lynnwood who did not know of her capabilities?

Inae Piercy has known Nicola Smith for many years. Piercy said, "Nicola's style of leadership was needed in the City of Lynnwood. She listens, she acts and she is very fair." Piercy first met Nicola and her husband Del when they brought their daughter Tia to the Soundview School in the Fourth Grade. She later re-met Nicola and Del in Rotary. Piercy has been the membership chair, community service chair, international committee for the Rotary Club. "Nicola wasn't thinking of running for mayor," Piercy said. "Jean Hales, who was committed to getting good leadership in place, told Nicola with great urgency: 'You need to run!'"

Chapter 3
A Winning Team

Theresa Poalucci knows everything about Nicola Smith and her family. Theresa first met Nicola in Rotary. There were four women who were fairly new to the Lynnwood Rotary Club, all of whom hit it off and became fast friends. Theresa owned the Journal Newspapers (13 community newspapers covering news in the Puget Sound area); one woman was vice president of a bank; another woman owned a travel business; and, at the time, Nicola was a dean of student life and development at Edmonds College. The four women often took trips together. Theresa remembers saying to her husband, "I'm going to San Francisco. See you in a couple of days." Of the four women, Theresa and Nicola became very close and often think of themselves as sisters.

They started including their spouses on trips, Theresa's husband, David and Nicola's husband, Del. Once a year they took a vacation together. Sometimes they brought their daughters. The spring of 2013 took the two couples on a road trip to New Mexico, traveling north from Tucson through to Sedona and Red Rock country, where formations glowed orange and red in the ever-changing sunlight from dawn to dusk. Traveling on the old Route 66, they made their way to the national monument Canyon de Chelly that had long served as a home for the Navajo people until it was invaded by troops led by Lt. Antonio Narbona in 1805. None of the history of this monument was lost on Nicola. She was slowly realizing that the connection the Navajo had to this land was the same way she was rooted in Lynnwood. She cared deeply about the community she had come to know in the city she had made home.

The idea of Nicola running for mayor was first floated around at Rotary about four years ago, but it was put on hold. Theresa recalls that when a number of people, Jean Hales and others, approached Nicola to ask her to run for mayor, she did think about it, but there was some apprehension.

On the road trip, they were traveling through wide open stretches of rocky land, naturally harsh and dry, barren but beautiful, especially when they encountered the natural dwellings of the Navajo. It was while traveling through this magical terrain that Nicola spoke about running for mayor. She told Theresa she was going to run. She also told her she was really nervous about having to make speeches. Theresa told her she would have to make plenty of speeches if she was going to be mayor. As they traveled through the desert in a loop to head back to Tucson, they made a giant circle, passing the time to write the press releases that would launch her campaign.

Soon, Nicola received many phone calls encouraging her to run. She first met with Edmonds College President Jean Hernandez, Edmonds Mayor Dave Earling, and other local leaders to see what she was getting into.

Having first met Nicola in 2011, **Jean Hernandez** describes Nicola as having a very rich history with the college. "She has an unbelievable amount of love and energy. She had a number of students who still kept close contact even after they left the college. She called me when she knew she was going to put her name in to run for mayor. I was excited because of the opportunities for partnership with someone in the city who knew the college."

Jean Hernandez's words about the potential for partnership between the city and the college later proved to be prophetic. As Nicola's vision of the job as mayor began to take shape, the relationship between the city and the college strengthened on many fronts, ranging from transportation to the development of student housing.

Edmonds Mayor **Dave Earling** had not met Nicola Smith when she was a dean at Edmonds College. He had gotten a call from a friend who was going to help with her campaign. He asked Mayor Earling to meet with her to help give her a sense of what she might face. He remembers being concerned because while she was an administrator who had done a fine job, she didn't speak the same language as more seasoned elected officials. Nor did she have the same standards and expectations that one might have when you're in politics, instead of when you're running an institution.

Still, he found her to be thoughtful and engaging.

"In the first meeting, I found her to be straightforward, a great listener, friendly, but not trying to overpower or impress. She was also smart and a quick study," Mayor Earling said. "She also took the advice from lots of people, and organized a group of folks she could rely on so that she could understand the modulation of going from a college setting to a political office."

To effectively run for mayor, one of the first things Nicola Smith needed was a campaign manager. **Ean Olsen** remembers knowing her when they were both working at Edmonds College. At the time, Ean was student administrative liaison and Nicola was the dean of student services. She made an indelible impression on him. "The really big thing she had was accessibility," he said. She stood up for the students. She made it so the athletic department was getting what it needed and the arts department was going through big changes. We lost our drama department. She was there to listen, and to be there for everyone throughout the entire process." After Ean left Edmonds College he went on to major in political science and cultural anthropology at Western Washington University. He heard she was running for mayor and contacted her. Ean said he had needed Nicola while he was at the college and now the tables had turned—she needed him as her campaign manager.

Nicola Smith and Ean Olsen were both new to the political campaign trail. There was no time to lose and every opportunity to think outside of the box to find innovative ways to reach the community. Ean said, "It was fun to have the familiarity of having worked with each other, then dive into the politics in a city we both knew and lived in."

Traditionally, canvassing is done to have direct contact with the electorate during a political campaign and involves grassroots fundraising, membership drives and raising community awareness. It also means knocking on doors and doorbelling to contact people at home. By canvassing neighborhoods and talking to people, Ean had the understanding that the Lynnwood community felt it was time for a change. Lynnwood needed a fresh perspective and a lot of administrative experience. The mayoral campaign tagline was ***Refresh and Reset***.

Ean Olsen and Nicola Smith turned canvassing on its ear by going on the road with a "pop-up listening tour." They pitched a tent, took a table and chairs, a popcorn machine and a whiteboard. "Nicola had always shown previous ability to listen, so we did a real listening tour." Nicola took her finely honed instinct to listen and turned it into the art of listening well.

Judge Jeffrey Goodwin commented on Nicola's ability to listen. "One of the things I have tremendous respect for is her ability to communicate. She's an amazing listener. She has the ability to be involved in a conversation. Whenever you're in a conversation she makes you feel that this is an important conversation. There is a sincerity there."

Theresa Poalucci remembers the pop-up tents where the whiteboard was transformed into a wish list of what people envisioned for their city. She remembers Nicola greeting people in her tent. "She was easy to approach and nothing is intimidating to her." She went from neighborhood to neighborhood popping up in parks and parking lots in a traveling road show. She asked people want they wanted. What did they wish for? "I remember I wrote that I wanted a dog park," Theresa said. "As it turned out a lot of people wanted to have a dog park. They got a dog park."

Making promises that she would deliver had always been at the core of Nicola Smith's persona, but her lack of political experience quickly became a point of attack as the mayoral campaign grew more heated. Incumbent Don Gough had been the mayor of Lynnwood since 2005.

Anyone who knew Nicola at Edmonds College knew of her leadership capabilities. **Andrew Ballard**, who is the chief growth strategist and principal of the firm Marketing Solutions, had a chance to see her leadership style up close and personal before she left the college. He met Nicola when he first joined the Lynnwood Rotary Club—that is when she was one of the deans at Edmonds

College. When she became president of the Rotary, she asked him to lead strategic planning. "I just love her leadership style. She's smart, a good listener and inclusive; she wants to hear other voices." Ballard sought her counsel on more than one occasion because he respected her leadership. While she was president of the Rotary Club, she took the time to mentor Andrew Ballard.

Kyle Funakoshi was aware of her commitment to her staff and students at Edmonds College. The relationships she built there lasted for years beyond her jobs with the college. Kyle Funakoshi developed programs that helped students from historically marginalized communities to succeed at Edmonds College. His job, in large part, was to serve students who were coming from low-income communities. "Nicola had a passion for working with these communities," he said. "If she didn't understand the issues, she was always willing to sit down and learn." At that time, Nicola was his boss's boss. "She was helping all communities to succeed, and she knew how to get things done. She's a true leader in every sense of the word."

Wally Webster, chair of the board of trustees at Edmonds College, was also her campaign manager in 2016. "Convincing her that running for mayor was the right thing to do—leaving her students at college—was a difficult decision," he said. Going back to when she first ran for Mayor in 2013, he cited the greatest challenge that Nicola faced was the fact that she did not have any experience in government. This required courage and support that would not necessarily come from the city council."

The support for Nicola's campaign did indeed come from other important influencers in the city who saw her character attributes and work habits that prepared her for the role as mayor. "Nicola's main strengths are her people skills," George Smith said. "She hired good people, nurtured those people and was an excellent mentor. She knew how to organize teams, collaborate and get the job done. All of those skills transferred over very well to her success as mayor. She had all of the skills necessary to be a good civic leader."

Kyle Funakoshi noted, "When you're an effective leader, some people wonder how is that working? Some might envy those leadership qualities, but she was able to manage all of that."

For 26 years, **Kevin McKay** worked together with Nicola Smith in different capacities at Edmonds College. In April 2020, he retired as the VP for finance and operations at the college and is now living on the stunningly beautiful Portuguese island of Madeira. He remembers that he and Nicola started working at the college at close to the same time. Through the years, he had plenty of time to observe her character, even in tough situations. In his estimation, she had the key attributes that would unquestionably allow her to become a successful mayor.

"She was visionary, always looking forward, seeking a better way to better serve students and improve the process of how things got done. She was also collaborative, very good at bringing teams of people together to solve challenges. She listened well to other voices and opinions and always sought to find the best path forward. Determined and persistent, she had little patience for unnecessary roadblocks or for people who obstruct processes. If necessary, she will drive forward and find new pathways, working with others who also desire progress and change."

McKay uses the student housing project, Rainier Place, as a great example of how Nicola's qualities guided her to push a difficult project steadily forward despite several unforeseen challenges. The economic climate at the time was not favorable for building such a project. "Most colleges would have given up on the project, especially since student housing was a ground-breaking concept for community colleges at that time," he said. "With her combination of being visionary, collaborative and determined, she has a true heart for people and that shows in the initiatives she has worked hardest to bring to fruition."

Faimous Harrison, who also came to first know Nicola at Edmonds College, mentions how she had the ability to look at issues through another person's lens. He thinks the way she interacts with different people helps her to grow, but her capacity for leadership grows as well.

"We did some deep dives to figure out how we could be a more inclusive campus. We started a wheelchair basketball club and participated with the community. Nicola wanted to improve the equity between our female and male athletes and sports teams and supported the transition of the baseball field (in need of a lot of work) to become a beautiful women's and men's multisports complex that also included softball and soccer. She always wanted to understand how the things we did have an impact on people."

"We did some deep dives to figure out how we could be a more inclusive campus. We had a wheelchair basketball club and participated with the community. We had a baseball field that needed work and she helped to improve it. She always wanted to understand how the things we did have an impact on people."

If you ask Faimous Harrison how he first came to meet Nicola Smith at Edmonds College, he is quick to say, "I've known Nicola for close to 20 years. She brought me in from South Seattle Community College. She has always been a risk-taker," he said, adding a small laugh. Faimous had been originally hired as the athletic director. Nicola was also his supervisor. "She was the dean of student services. That was how I originally met her. She also became the women's commissioner for sporting events. I was the men's commissioner. We traveled together."

He especially remembers the trip to India. Nicola was the team lead in a five-person group for a Rotary service project. Faimous had been selected to participate as an administrative fellow on the trip. The Group Study Exchange is the Rotary Foundation's most important international development program for young professionals who are non-Rotarians.

"We had meetings and prep before our travel because we would be living with host families and representing the United States," Faimous said. "We had a lot of obligations, doing presentations, visiting hospitals and schools, we were focused on socio-economic disparities. It was a transformational experience. I realized I would never be the same."

In retrospect, he sees how his experience in India shaped his life and helped him to see how leadership makes a difference in people's lives. He still remembers Nicola giving polio vaccine drops to children. He saw a level of poverty that he had never imagined and wanted to become a person who understands humility and placing service above self.

"I'm very appreciative to Nicola for giving us an understanding of leadership."

Today Faimous Harrison is still in higher education and has been dean of the Stockton Campus at California State University since 2016. He spends a lot of time focusing on leadership. "People who get in leadership positions often forget how they got there," he said. "Nicola learns from others' journeys, successes and failures. She has a leadership that you can be confident that she will make the best decisions to support the people."

Today **Jorge de la Torre** is the dean for student success/student engagement at Edmonds College. (Ironically, this was Nicola's former position at Edmonds College.) Jorge shares a funny story about how he first met Nicola. George Smith was vice president, Jean Hernandez was president, and Nicola was the chair of the hiring committee. Jorge was recruited from San Diego to fly into Seattle to meet them in Lynnwood for an interview. Jorge's third daughter had just arrived a few days before and he had not slept much before the interview. He was alarmed because someone told him he was late for the interview. Off his game, he rattled responses to the interview questions but did not feel as though he was doing a very good job. "Sometimes in an interview, you remember connecting with people and you remember not connecting with a few people," he said. "I remember looking at Nicola the whole time because she nodded with reassurance and smiled, and that gave me confidence." Jorge found himself rallying in the second half of the interview.

He also asked Nicola if George Smith was her husband. In ordinary circumstances that might be considered to be a gaffe, but in this case, he learned that although Nicola Smith and George Smith were not related, her husband Del Smith really did work at the college!

When Jorge found out she was running for mayor, he knew she would do a good job.

"I knew no matter what she did, she had a vision." When she had talked about Rainier Place, the housing on campus—she was the most key person to get the building built. She was responsible for getting Triton Field built, and for getting the student union built. The way I think she did it is because she is a real connector, connecting different departments together and different parts of the community.

Although Nicola's background had demonstrated a long track record at the college of managing multiple departments and programs with competing interests and complex budgets, the incumbent mayor, Don Gough, appeared to be amused by her candidacy and deemed her to be unqualified. And even though Gough didn't garner anywhere near a sizable majority during the primary, he seemed pleased enough at the results. "We're ready to move on to the general election," Gough said at that time. "I'm happy with where we're at." Gough then reportedly said he planned to take a break from the campaign trail to spend time with his family.

Theresa Poalucci remarked how even though Nicola's knowledge about city government was limited, the group thought she had a great chance. When Poalucci defined "the group," she meant the Lynnwood Rotary Club. Most of the people in Rotary are business owners. "A hundred people adored Nicola and there was a lot of strength in that number," Poalucci said. "Nicola had been president of Rotary. All of her folks from the college and all of the Rotarians, everyone knew she was a great administrator. There was a lot of support behind her to run for mayor."

Wally Webster agrees. "Her greatest advantage was being open and listening to the advice that was given. Her willingness to listen is what made her a successful candidate. She had this very diverse group of people who advised her of the next steps and strategy." Nicola Smith and Ean Olsen became a winning team, ending the reign of two-term incumbent Mayor Don Gough. "We just figured it out together," Olsen said.

Smith had 61.4% or 2,076 votes. Gough had 1,284 votes, or just under 38%. This election was much more than the unraveling of small-town politics. It was a race between the old and the new, and an indicator of what happens when a small city is marked for growth and destined to become a regional leader in Puget Sound. Upon winning the election in a landslide, Nicola Smith said, "I am really honored to be in this position and I'm very excited that the voters have entrusted me to move our city forward.

Chapter 4
Becoming Mayor Smith

Nicola Smith was sworn in as the mayor of Lynnwood by Municipal Court Judge Stephen Moore during the Dec. 9, 2013, Lynnwood City Council meeting. The sky was full of the dark dense clouds of December. Although the temperature hovered just above freezing at 34 degrees, the damp air made it feel colder. The swearing-in ceremony was brief on this Monday night, partially because this was the last day the city council would meet for the year. Although her new job wouldn't officially begin until January 1, there was much groundwork to be laid to chart the course for the road ahead.

"After the November Election it sunk in that I was going to be the next mayor of Lynnwood. By the time I was sworn in the only anxiety I had was being in front of a real live judge for the first time in my life! A very large crowd filled the council chambers that evening and so I was surrounded by positive vibes and a celebratory spirit. The oath was the end of what I call a six-month job interview process by the people and I must have done a pretty good job because here I was getting sworn in."

Mayor Nicola Smith beamed with the sort of pride that made her exuberant because she couldn't quite believe all that had transpired in such a short time. The campaign became "this overwhelming grassroots support that just ballooned and really gave me the energy and enthusiasm," she told the press. And she couldn't wait to get to work.

Since her return from Haiti the week before, she had already been talking to the city department directors, staff and other key influencers in the community. The whiteboard she had used on the campaign trail during her "pop-up listening tour" had evolved into a long list of issues that the city needed to address.

She had already been hearing rumors about who she planned to hire and fire at City Hall. She knew it was not that simple. She needed to get to know the city employees to figure out what was working and what was not working. She knew there would be some shuffling of personnel, placing the best people in the jobs where they would set a new standard of excellence.

As Mayor of Lynnwood, Nicola Smith was responsible for coordinating and directing the overall administration of all city departments, including Administrative Services, Community Development, Economic Development, Executive, Fire Department, Human Resources, Information Technology, Parks and Recreation, Police Department and Public Works.

As the administrative head of the city government, she was responsible for the overall management of all city functions and services by implementing city council policies and directives, and by providing Intergovernmental coordination and city representation. She was the liaison between the city council and staff, was responsible for budget preparation and implementation, regular and special reports, and the coordination of the activities of various departments.

There was a lot to learn.

An elected, seven-member council serves staggered, four-year terms, meaning that the election of council members takes place every two years. The seven members of the Lynnwood City Council are elected at-large to serve for four-year terms. Each year the council elects a President and a Vice President from within the council. Some of the city council's primary duties are to make laws, adopt regulations and budgets, levy taxes, authorize public improvements, provide for Public Safety and health, approve board and commission appointments, and oversee a wide-ranging agenda for the people of Lynnwood. All business of the council is conducted in public, except for Executive Session items such as property acquisition, personnel issues and potential litigation. The council confirms the mayor's appointments of management to oversee the city's daily operations, as well as its approximately 373 full-time employees and 130 part-time employees.

Rev. M. Christopher Boyer recalls working with Mayor Smith and some of the other council members as good experiences. "When Nicola came along, I didn't know her before. It was clear that she honestly cared about the people who she represented. We worked very well together for four years."

With an extensive background in Public Safety, **Shannon Sessions** has served on the Lynnwood City Council since 2015 and is currently in the second year of her second term.

Sessions recalls Nicola consulting with her when she was first asked to run for mayor. Sessions thought Mayor Smith was helped by her lack of political experience. "She led with the heart and that is what the employees and community needed, and it was necessary to grow a regional presence because that was lost in the past."

Past Lynnwood City Council member from Jan 2012 to December 2015, **Sid Roberts** was also council vice president in 2013-2014. He later served on the planning commission for the city of Stanwood and also served on the Stanwood City Council. Today he is also a board member of Community Transit. "When I was there, her relationship with the city council was very good. She's one of those people that it would be hard to be cross with. She doesn't push buttons. She's a strong person, remarkably resilient and capable. She doesn't lead with insecurity but leads with a calmness that helps other people relax. When I was there, her relationship with the council was very good."

For many years any sort of relationship between the top leadership in the City of Lynnwood and civic leaders in Snohomish County as well as in the state of Washington had been missing in action. With the plans for the light rail coming to Lynnwood, Mayor Smith knew she needed to work regionally with other cities. Regional collaboration meant working with the other mayors of Snohomish County as well as with the Snohomish County Executive, the Snohomish County Council, several state representatives and the U.S. congressional representative for the 32nd and 21st Districts. Working collaboratively in the region required much more than forging relationships with elected officials; it also meant forming relationships with a whole host of individuals from both the private and public sectors. Under Mayor Smith's leadership, Lynnwood was about to undergo a transformation from being perceived as a small town to becoming a regional leader.

Since the election, Nicola had been mostly been thinking about what's next. The first priority would be to focus on changing from the inside out. One thing was certain, "I want to see a new culture in city hall," she said.

She immediately set about creating an effective way to communicate to the community. She was astonished to learn that the city didn't have anyone doing communications. The prior administration did not want to talk to the community.

In her conversation with **Lynn Sordel,** the Director of Parks and Recreation, she learned of a young woman, **Julie Moore**, who had been effectively doing communication for the Parks Department. Her job was officially classified as an Outreach Specialist, but her role had not been fully formed. Lynn Sordel said, "She's already doing this work," and suggested to Mayor Smith that she give her a shot by moving her into the position as the city's Public Affairs Officer.

In Julie Moore's opinion, "Mayor Smith trusted me and thought I was connected to the community, the city staff and the volunteers. She gave me a lot of leeway to figure it out and do what's beneficial to the community."

Julie recalls Mayor Smith always asking for her assessment of the issues that arose. "Tell me what you think?" Moore felt empowered by the fact that the mayor recognized her talent and her growing communications expertise.

Speaking of *Mayor,* she had always been called *Nicola* by everyone: family, friends, business associates and colleagues alike. According to Julie Moore, "She didn't want to be called Mayor Smith; she felt like it was too pretentious, it wasn't who she was, but I insisted, I told her, 'Being the mayor is a big deal, you have to own it!'"

In her new role, Moore continued to do outreach work, the same as before, but her role expanded further into strategic communications and public affairs. Moore acknowledges the high standards that she has set for herself. "Something that we constantly hear is 'we should communicate more'. There is never enough communication—that's the hard thing. We can always do more."

The decision to create the Public Affairs Officer proved to be not only wise but pragmatic. One of Moore's projects was to implement the city's online presence: website, social media and electronic newsletters. Having this communication infrastructure in place later became an effective tool for everyday communications and in times of crisis, especially the pandemic in 2020. "I was in the right place at the right time. I'm so thankful for Nicola's trust in me," Moore said. "I think we're doing a great job of communicating and engaging."

The whiteboard concept that Mayor Smith used in her campaign became more than a list of issues, but among the staff members at City Hall it had taken on a new name, the "Fix it List." Mayor Smith wanted to implement lean processes to improve efficiency and service. "How do we make things better?" she asked. "We want the people who are doing the work to tell us how to make it better."

Corbitt Loch was put in charge of the "Fix it List." His working job title was senior manager of strategic planning, a varied position. The city had a biennial budget. In even-numbered years, Corbitt Loch was one of the leads in developing the city's budget, a full time gig. In odd-numbered years, he did more strategic planning work and took on many aspects of process improvement, efficiency studies, organizational development, legislation and policy analysis. He considers himself to be a rover. "I go where needed to improve the city as an organization," Loch said.

To say that the City of Lynnwood was not progressive as an administrative work culture is being polite. The city administration was mired in a lot of regulations and policies that were no longer the best choice. The mayor heard (as she came in) that every department had areas where they needed to retool—to become as current and as productive as possible. "She understood that we needed many, many big and little changes," Loch said. "As for the Fix it List, it was prudent to log these changes, to keep track of them, and to see our progress." Of the hundred things on this list, Loch estimates that 80% of them were changed. "One by one, these changes were made," he said. "The mayor was a change agent."

The Administrator of the Mayor's Office is essentially the mayor's deputy, or Chief of Operations for day-to-day functioning and works closely with the city council. **Art Ceniza** had held this post long enough to have served under two mayors, including Mayor Smith. In his estimation, Lynnwood was going through a crisis. The city was just coming out of the Great Recession of 2008, beginning to recover to where it was before the recession, and still searching for stability in its revenues. Mayor Smith brought a sense of calm and relief to the city's staff. Ceniza detected from day one that she didn't have any sort of agenda to position herself for the next higher office. She wasn't interested in making politics a career. No one knew her. Ceniza had not known her until now.

"She had a really big impact from day one because she outlined a vision of good things. She was very empowering with her staff and very collaborative," Ceniza said. "She allowed her staff to speak candidly without being retaliated against."

Ceniza thought the new mayor genuinely sought the advice of the professional government workers, people like Ceniza, who had been on staff for a while and had that experience to bring to the table. She did not pretend to know it all. "She truly utilized the expertise of her staff." She wasn't there to get more votes or to get reelected. He thought she was intent on doing the right thing.

City Clerk **Karen Fitzhum** joined the staff about a month after Mayor Smith began her first term. She did not know the new mayor before she took office. Fitzhum had been concerned about going to Lynnwood. "I didn't know if the incoming mayor meant what she said or if she was full of beans." At that time, the city administration was at an all-time low. No one knew what to expect. Fitzhum saw good people hesitating before doing anything. In her past positions, she had observed city clerks who would hide when they saw their mayor or council members walk into the room. They made themselves scarce. There was a significant amount of that going on.

"They were in a Post-Traumatic Stress syndrome situation," she said.

Making change in an organization is hard to accomplish. Art Ceniza speaks of the tremendous trust and the ability to bring people together that Mayor Smith brought to the table. Setting forth this new tone of leadership was critical at the time when she took office. "There was great tension and not a whole lot of trust. She had to mend that bridge," Ceniza said. "Mayor Smith actually modeled that behavior and quickly became trusted by people on both sides of the fence."

The change in the city's work culture has been dramatic, Karen Fitzhum concurs. "The number of people I'm working with today worked in the previous administration when it was difficult." Fitzhum was on the lean team and worked on ways to improve processes and streamline efficiency. "We respect one another. We're kind to one another."

The mayor's physical office became an outward symbol of the transformation of the city's administrative culture. The prior mayor's office space was dark and gloomy. Heavy draperies covered the windows so no one could see in and no one could look out. Huge mounds of files were piled on all the desktops, all over the floor and were stuffed onto the surface of every nook and cranny. The staff had worked hard to get the office cleaned out. Mayor Smith remembers Johnie, the maintenance supervisor, calling her to ask her what color she wanted the walls painted, what did she want on the floor, which way did she want the doors to open, what type of window treatments did she want, and what did she want to be hung on the walls. "The staff was yearning for a refresh and reset, not only for a mayor but for the workplace environment."

Johnie and his crew built a desk made from reclaimed wood that was sourced from an old tree that had fallen in the city hall courtyard. The desk's frame was constructed from old shelving that came from the IT department, and its legs were made from old library tables. The walls were painted mint green to evoke creativity and the dark molding was transformed into bright white. "I worked on making my office a place that would feel like anyone's living room."

Her friend Theresa Poalucci created a large painting, *The Stand of Trees*, depicting Mayor Smith's theme for leading the city: 13 long trunk trees, exposing their roots and their overhead canopy. Each trunk symbolized all of the city's departments, the city council, the commissions and boards and the City of Lynnwood community. "The roots bound us together as a strong foundation and as we grew together in order to make Lynnwood flourish. This was the beginning of working with city leadership to work together as 'One Lynnwood.'"[1]

Mayor Smith was determined to create a safe environment where her staff felt empowered to do their best work. This change made in the internal city work culture was also intended to spread outside to the entire community. She wanted Lynnwood to feel more welcoming to the people who lived and worked there. She also knew that she was operating under the constraints of the city's two-year budget that had already been predetermined. The police and fire departments both had imminent needs and the city was still hurting from the economic downturn. She saw the changes that needed to be made. She could have kept things the way they were but recognized change needed to be made because it was the right thing to do. *"How do we make it better? How do we listen?"* are the two questions she often asked of herself and everyone else.

---

[1] The Stand of Trees by Artist Theresa Poalucci can be viewed on her website: https://www.artisttheresapoalucci.com/

Chapter 5
The Strategic Vision for the City

As both a public servant and a leader, Mayor Smith would provide the guidance and support for the development of effective programs, and the planning, evaluation, analysis, control, and general management of the programs. Those who made light of her background as a mere administrator in education were soon in for a surprise. Her detractors had not looked at the sheer weight of her credentials. Aside from having a Masters of Education from Western Washington University, and a bachelor's degree from the University of Washington, she also held Certificates from FEMA, Emergency Operations training, Threat Assessment Team training, Safe Zone Facilitator, Ally Training, and Client Service Contracts from OFM, Dependable Strengths.

The detailed development plan that Jean Hales had referenced had indeed been created long ago but had never gotten off the ground. One of the first things Mayor Smith did was to examine plans dating back to 2001. The plan for the development of the downtown city center was full of good intentions but had never been brought to fruition due to poor management and leadership. The stalled projects and projects that had been thought about but never had a chance to be implemented now stood to have a second chance.

During those early days in her new role, Mayor Smith did more than listen to her staff. She also knew how to ask the right questions to get the root of the problem. Andrew Ballard observed that if you define the core attributes of an effective leader, you will find a picture of Nicola Smith. "If there is a problem," Ballard said. "She will bring all of the parties involved into the same room to hash it out. She is also a very good mediator. She's purposeful and what she does is well thought out."

A new plan emerged that defined *The Five Priorities* for the City of Lynnwood:
> The City Center and the Light Rail,
> Financial Stability and Economic Success,
> Operational and Organizational Success,
> Public Safety (creating a safe and livable city),
> and the need for Collaboration/Partnerships.

The City Center and the Light Rail

Historically, Lynnwood had been behind other cities in terms of serving its population's transportation needs, but no longer. With the light rail expansion to Lynnwood, the race to the future was on. Ensuring that the City of Lynnwood was prepared for the explosion of growth was Mayor Smith's chief priority. She knew that this surge of unprecedented growth would impact every facet of the city and everyone who lived or worked there. "I am very excited that the light rail is coming through Lynnwood!" she said.

It was very important that the people who live and work in Lynnwood had a way to get to the University of Washington or downtown Seattle in a timely manner: 12 minutes to the University of Washington, 24 minutes to downtown Seattle. The light rail would be an enhancement for the people who want to have access to the opportunities that Seattle offers, without having to get stuck in traffic on the freeway. At that time, the Seattle Metropolitan area was often cited as having one of the worst traffic problems in the country.

By taking the heat off the freeways and arterials and speeding up commute time, the growth of Lynnwood was inevitable; the population would increase tremendously. Much of the city's current building stock had been built during the 1960s and 1970s. The community's "downtown" had shifted over the last several decades, from the Interurban station in Alderwood Manor in the 1930s, to Highway 99 after World War II, to the Alderwood Mall area after its construction in the 1970s.

Now another shift would occur. There needed to be an increase in housing development. There also needed to be accessible local transportation to and from the downtown city center core to other parts of the city. The development of a downtown city center would no longer be stalled. Mayor Nicola was prepared to meet the needs of the growing city by working to bring together the right people who could create sustainable development for the future.

Financial Stability and Economic Success

The city had been trying to survive financially for many years. The Great Recession of 2008 resulted in many budget restraints and cutbacks. By 2013 the city still had not recovered. Businesses were unwilling to relocate to Lynnwood and developers were not keen on developing new properties because of the complicated business application and permit process that was widely known to be fraught with delays, incompetence and frustration. There was great turnover in staff and great turmoil. There was also a lack of trust among department heads. Overall, there was a lack of financial leadership and transparency. Mayor Smith immediately examined which elements needed to be in place to ensure the city's financial success.

Ensuring financial stability and economic success were two areas of administration that were joined at the hip, and yet a two-pronged approach was needed. For years the city had been plagued with getting poor ratings based on the standards set forth by the Government Accounting Standards Board (GASB.) Established in 1984, the GASB (known colloquially as *Gasbee*) is a private, non-governmental organization. GASB is the source of generally accepted accounting principles used by state and local governments in the United States. As with most of the entities involved in creating generally accepted accounting principles in the United States, GASB provides the accounting rules for government entities. All current accounting rules must be implemented. Accounting rules are Federally regulated through GASB. It is the job of GASB auditors to find if anything is wrong. For years, the City of Lynnwood had large errors in its financial reporting. These findings resulted in poor audits, and that impacted the city's municipal bond ratings.

Mayor Smith saw the imminent need for fiscal stewardship and transparency. What had been happening and what needed to be changed? The city could not realize economic success unless its internal financial oversight was stabilized and improved.

Organizational Success

Economic and business growth was stalled for many years. Organizational changes needed to be made. Mayor Smith wanted to improve the entire city organization, by engaging staff at all levels and matching the right staff with the right jobs that needed to be done. The new operative mandates were efficiency, innovation and transparency. Changing the city's internal work culture to improve the customer experience required the hiring, firing and shifting of personnel. The overarching message that Mayor Smith wanted to deliver to the business community was *Lynnwood is Open for Business*.

"Making change is harder to do than not making change," **Corbitt Loch** said. "Organizations, especially governments, are always designed to create uniformity and consistency in how they do their work and how they impact citizens. Creating rules is part of that DNA. To change those rules is almost contrary to the DNA. And you have human beings. Many people are change adverse. People are creatures of habit. They do what they know and like and shy away from things that are different."

Another reason for resistance to organizational change is political. Elected officials tend not to be comfortable with making radical change, primarily because their emphasis is going to be on getting reelected. This would turn out not to be the case with Mayor Smith. According to Loch, "She could have kept things the way they are, but she recognized the changes that needed to be made because it was the right thing to do."

Public Safety

The realm of Public Safety included much more than keeping Lynnwood's citizens safe from crime, fire, natural disasters, inadequate roads and traffic congestion. Public safety also encompassed protecting the health and well-being of the community, as well as making the city welcoming and inclusive to everyone.

With the anticipated influx of new residents and commuters, Mayor Smith recognized that the increasing diversification of the city meant that the growing needs of the community had to be anticipated and accommodated.

From a purely practical standpoint, the city's core Public Safety services, The Fire Department, the Police Department and the Departments of Public Works and Parks, had to be examined for what was working, and what was not working. More importantly, these departments had to be assessed for what was needed to be in place to accommodate the changing population. The city needed to have the governance in place to make sure that Lynnwood's growth was healthy and positive and a connection to the community was established to create safety for all of its citizens.

Collaboration/Partnerships
The need for collaboration and the formation of strategic partnerships can never be overstated or overlooked. Collaboration and partnerships are critical to leveraging the city's resources in order to achieve the greatest outcome possible. Early on, in order to support the business community, Mayor Smith recognized the need for the city to develop business partnerships with the Lynnwood Chamber of Commerce and the Snohomish County Economic Alliance.

The impending expansion of the light rail also gave Lynnwood the opportunity to become a regional model for growth. Other collaborative relationships would emerge with Sound Transit, Community Transit, the Verdant Health Commission, Edmonds College, Homage-Senior Services, and a wide range of community organizations and interest groups. Additionally, relationships needed to be forged with city, county and state representatives—the entire network of elected officials in the region.

Senator Marko Liias, who represents the communities of the 21st Legislative District, which includes neighborhoods in Edmonds, Everett, Lynnwood and Mukilteo, said, "Becoming a collaborative regional leader doesn't happen by accident. To be that leader at a regional level takes effort and intention and must be done by the right person." Mayor Smith was exactly the right person in the right place at the right time. Sen. Liias said, "Nicola has thrown open the doors to city government."

No discussion about collaboration and partnerships would be complete unless it is noted just how important Mayor Smith thought it was for the city to serve its community. She thought it was more important than ever for citizens to serve at a grassroots level where they can create long-term positive results in their communities. She fully intended for a diversity initiative of unprecedented magnitude to permeate the city's culture from both inside and out. Her "All Are Welcome" initiative became more than a message but a mandate guiding the road map to create the Lynnwood of the future.

Chapter 6
Fiscal Stewardship

As Finance Director for the City of Lynnwood from 2011 to 2014, **Lorenzo Hines** recalls the fiscal health of the city at that time as being questionable. The city was still struggling with coming out of the Great Recession of 2008 and the general fund balance was pretty low. He notes that there were entities, essentially banks, who were waiting for the city to declare bankruptcy. "Those were hard days," he said, "but we got through it." He makes it clear that the city's executive team knew the details about the fiscal situation and was able to work with plans to reduce expenditures. He feels that he gained the confidence of the city council, and the former Mayor Don Gough.

The official duties that Hines oversaw included oversight of the city's accounting, budgets, financial reporting, utility billing, payroll, accounts payable and investing funds, as well as, overseeing information technology (IT). In his words, his unofficial duties "were to fill the leadership vacuum and to be the liaison between the council and a mayor…to try to get things to move forward, despite their complicated relationship." He was not alone in his efforts to move forward. "Art Ceniza was there with me as well," Hines said.

Art Ceniza came on board as city administrator in 2010. Ceniza recalls the time before Mayor Smith as being a very challenging situation. "When there is that much tension, there is no trust." The tensions grew so high and the trust was so low that an outside consultant was hired to help remedy the situation. After evaluating the situation, the consultant wasn't sure he could help. According to Ceniza, the consultant said, "You're dysfunctional. You need a new team."

As the Director of Finance, Lorenzo Hines had found himself stuck in the midst of warring factions, trying to get different entities to work together. Some of the duties he was doing fell into the realm of being a city manager. "I realized that this was the appropriate career path for me." He left the City of Lynnwood to take a job with the California Secretary of State and later became the assistant city manager for the City of Pacifica, California. Today he is the city manager for the city of Galt, California. "I have Lynnwood to thank for my current career trajectory," he said.

From the moment Mayor Smith cast a sharp eye toward the city's Finance Department things began to change and a new era of fiscal stewardship was ushered into city hall. She said, "It seemed that the Finance Department was headed by the past mayor, so my biggest concern was that the department did not have the necessary experience to carry on as the city's finance leaders. A clean audit had not happened for many years and I needed to lead the finance group through all the fiscal clean up and build a skilled and talented leadership team to get us to a clean audit and sustainable budgeting practices."

Corbitt Loch remembers how Mayor Smith deferred to her experts and trusted their advice. He described her as having a steady hand and of being a calming force. She understood near-term and long-term implications. Loch credits Mayor Smith for creating an environment where greater trust was created between the city council and the city's staff. Instead of being at cross purposes, Loch felt that the city's staff began to work closely with the city council to update policies that set new ground rules for normalcy. A new transparency was also created so everyone could know if the city was on the right track with its finances.

Mayor Smith was always highly supportive and looking for collaboration from everyone involved so they would succeed. She did a good job of hiring people in the Finance Department who were smart and competent, so a lot of trust was built. "All of these things worked together to calm the seas of financial unrest," Loch said. By establishing good policies and procedures the budgeting process began to become streamlined and made more transparent.

Adding new staff and recruiting the right people to fit the changing work culture of the Finance Department also made a huge difference. In Corbitt Loch's case, he was recruited from within and began emphasizing the city's focus on strategic planning. Originally, he had been hired by the old organization to work in Community Development, and that was a culture he could not fit into and did not want to fit into because it did not match his ethics or his public service expectations. He recalls that time as very uncomfortable and emotionally very hard. But there was a happy ending.

"The mayor saw something in me, and once she started to get to know me, she said, 'I could use somebody like you'—that's when in 2015, I came from Community Development and started working in strategic planning."

Corbitt Loch spoke highly of another major change in the Finance Department. "After 2015 it was really great. I had a great boss—Sonja Springer."

The new Finance Director, **Sonja Springer**, came on board in 2015. Before then, she had spent 32 years in municipal government finance, and from 2000 to 2015 she had been the Finance Director for the city of Mountlake Terrace. "I was happy at Mountlake Terrace, but I needed another challenge in my career and working with Mayor Smith was a great experience," she said. "I did not want to be with Lynnwood until Mayor Smith was there. I was never interested in becoming involved with Lynnwood, but when Mayor Smith came on board, I thought maybe I could do it this time."

She talks about why she became the Finance Director for the City of Lynnwood: "They needed help. That was a big reason why I moved from Mountlake Terrace. I wanted to achieve a standard of excellence for financial reporting. I also wanted to help them with their audits. There had been large errors in their financial reporting. I wanted them to improve their financial reporting that would allow them to get awards. I was determined to help them become a regional model for financial reporting and audits. To get them clean audits, they needed help."

As the Finance Director, Sonja Springer managed the biennial budget. "I was excited to get to Lynnwood because of the challenge," Springer said. The structure of a biennial budget had already been in place, which suited Springer because producing a budget every other year was more efficient. Otherwise, all summer long would be spent every year creating a budget and producing a financial outlook. She also oversaw all of the accounting and financial reports, monthly, quarterly and annual, utility billing, payroll, accounts payable, and investing funds so that the city receives the maximum amount of interest. She also managed a staff of 27 people.

When Springer came on board in June 2015, it was too late to put in controls needed to turn around the prospect of a less than perfect audit or an audit without findings. 2016 became the first year that the City of Lynnwood had a clean audit. "I had to change some staff to do that," Springer explained. "To get a good audit requires having good internal controls. It means that everybody knows their procedures and knows what they need to do and does it correctly." Controls have to be in place that reduce the number of errors and misuse so that there are not any errors in financial statements.

"People don't realize the State Auditor's Office is paid to oversee standards in municipal government," Springer said.

GASB puts out the rules and is the enforcer of those rules through the State Auditor's Office. They look at financial controls, the budget and the financial statements. They look at actual transactions to make sure the right people are being paid and that everything is being correctly recorded. Every year a state audit team starts in April and is not gone until August or September. Auditors are there to find things that could have happened. Their job is essentially to find anything wrong and to enforce the rules. Lynnwood has had the same audit team for a number of years.

Under Mayor Smith's leadership, the City of Lynnwood has had its first clean audit—with no findings—since 2008. In addition to the City of Lynnwood being given a clean financial bill of health, the invoice for Lynnwood's 2016 audit payment was $30,000 less than in 2015 due to the streamlined financial procedures that were now in place. Because Mayor Smith hired a professional and dedicated financial administrative services team, balance was restored to the city's budget and its government. Mayor Smith gave credit to her finance team. She said, "The finance team did incredible work to improve our accounting and financial reporting practices, to develop an innovative, results-oriented budget, and to bring greater transparency to the city finances."

Lynnwood made a turnaround. The city continued to receive clean audits for years, which had an impact on bond ratings. The city's municipal bond status went from A+ to AA+ in 2014 for general bonds and in 2015 for utility bonds. The AA+ designation indicates the City of Lynnwood has a very strong capacity to meet its financial commitments.[2] This rating is a sound predictor that the city is prepared to manage the growth ahead.

"Because of the good bond rating, the city will pay less in interest than if they had a bad rating. This saves the citizens of Lynnwood tax money," Springer said.

For the first time in many years, the city successfully submitted the city's 2016 Consolidated Annual Financial Report for a Government Financial Officers Association excellence in financial reporting award. The Municipal Research and Services Center for Washington State named Lynnwood's new 2016 financial policies as one of the three cities with 10,000-50,000 population as regional best practices. Going forward, the city administration has established the Economic Development Infrastructure Fund, funded by one-time, non-recurring revenues, which will be used to finance public infrastructure and public facilities as the city prepares for city center development and light rail in 2024.

"Mayor Smith lets the directors do what they need to do to achieve excellence in their departments," Springer said. "She let me run the Finance Department the way it needed to be run."

Having the right financial team in place to make sure the city was fiscally sound and fiscally responsible laid the groundwork for the change that the light rail would bring to the community. The city

---

[2] Lynnwood issued a bond in June, 2021. The bond's rating AA+ is a very strong rated bond, indicating a well run municipality. It is rated better than similar-sized municipalities in the state of Washington. Data derived from Morgan Stanley, New York City, July 28, 2021.

now had the proper governance in place to make sure that Lynnwood's growth was healthy, positive and created safety for the entire community. Under Mayor Smith's leadership, sweeping changes were already underway that would impact the five city departments—Fire, Parks, Police, Public Works and the Community Development—that worked to keep the community safe.

Chapter 7
Fire and Police Services

The safety of Lynnwood's citizens was the No. 1 priority for Mayor Smith. With the anticipated influx of new residents and commuters, the city would experience an increase in Public Safety needs, including fire and police department services. As a budget line item, a city's most significant outlays are often made to support its 24/7 fire and police department services. Lynnwood was no exception in this regard. The saga of Lynnwood's fire department services had two primary moving parts. For many reasons, mainly historical, Lynnwood was served by two fire departments: Fire District One and the City of Lynnwood Fire Department.

Fire District One had contracted with Mountlake Terrace, Edmonds and Brier. Only Mountlake Terrace and Edmonds had fire departments and a contract with Snohomish Fire District One that was previously in place. They disbanded their own city fire departments and remained a contract city with Snohomish Fire District One. After disbanding their own city fire departments, most of the employees went to Snohomish Fire District One. Since Snohomish Fire District One served the entire area surrounding Lynnwood, the city was often described colloquially as *the donut hole.*

The City of Lynnwood Fire Department was underfunded but well liked. Discussions of regionalization of fire service in Lynnwood began in 1972. Prior to Mayor Smith, talks to regionalize the fire department had stalled. There were attempts to do a consolidation multiple times over the years. A lot of people believed that a regional fire authority was a good process but, in the end, they were never able to bring it to a conclusion. People's positions, power and money were often cited as the chief obstacles that stood in the way of consolidation. Too many people were involved in these consolidation discussions, which made it a hugely complex task because so many people were trying to come to an agreement.

Mayor Smith recruited **Scott Cockrum** to become chief of the Lynnwood Fire Department. Cockrum had previously served at a county fire department for the Sacramento Region called the Sacramento Metropolitan fire department. Scott Cockrum also had extensive experience with fire department consolidations. While he was with Sacramento, originally there had been 16 different departments, but over time there were 14 consolidations. Scott Cockrum started with the City of Lynnwood at the end of 2014. Prior to then, in Sacramento, he was in a position in which he was going to retire or work a few more years with the possibility of being promoted to Fire Chief. He had reached a fork in the road and began exploring employment possibilities in several different cities.

The Seattle area appealed to Scott Cockrum. He had friends in the Woodinville area. Cockrum and Mayor Smith met for the first time during the interview process. "We didn't have previous knowledge of one another," Cockrum said. "I liked the mayor, and I liked the city. And I was high on her list to become the next fire chief. They offered me a job and I came and started working." Cockrum ended up staying with the Lynnwood Fire Department for almost three years.

When Chief Scott Cockrum first came on board, Mayor Smith was reasonably new in her position. According to Cockrum, she didn't have a strong opinion one way or another about a large regional consolidation effort. "I came in and never had a mandate to consolidate the fire department. I was there to run the Lynnwood Fire Department to find out what their current needs were, as well as to assess what their future needs would be."

In the meantime, Chief Cockrum was growing the Lynnwood Fire Department. "We modified how we responded to medical aids, and added resources to focus on collecting already approved transport fees. These changes resulted in increased revenue to the city, which we were able to use for needed equipment purchases. We were bringing the fire department into recovery." Cockrum said he was just starting to see revenues to turn around the department. The

Fire Department made changes to how they funded apparatus, the Emergency Medical Services delivery, and transports, which increased the department's revenue. "The Fire Department generated the revenue and felt inspired because it brought value back to our organization," Cockrum said.

Chief Scott Cockrum and Mayor Smith had many discussions about what the future would look like, specifically the Fire Department's response time, their capabilities and how well they integrated with corresponding Public Safety agencies. The inevitability of creating a single entity, a Regional Fire Authority became clear.

Merging two different entities to create a single Regional Fire Authority (RFA) was important to accomplish for several reasons. Having four or five different government entities running two station fire departments made the Public Safety aspect of service much more difficult. Several city councils were involved. Fire District One had its own board. It was difficult to coordinate a good fire delivery system when the decision-making process was spread over multiple entities. There is also duplication of effort and duplication of resources. Each city had its own Fire Chief, an Assistant Chief, a Training Division and a Fire Marshal. By consolidating, there is a reduction of some of the people holding authority positions, which helps to make better decisions that focus on the region instead of only on an individual city.

Another factor to consider is the cost of equipment. Each fire department maintained equipment. It's important to keep in mind that with the development of downtown Lynnwood, fire equipment would have to be upgraded and, in some instances, entirely new equipment would have to be purchased. High-rise housing requires a different fire response. Larger ladder trucks would need to be purchased to reach high-rise housing units. Fire trucks are expensive and cost up to $1 million.

"The cost to sustain the Lynnwood Fire Department would have continued to escalate due to the increased population growth and real estate development," Sonja Springer noted. The two fire departments were serving a fairly small area in Snohomish County.

Overall, the duplication of service tended to cause waste and increased the cost of doing business.

Beyond some people not wanting to give up their positions of authority, there was another major obstacle to the consolidation. In the City of Lynnwood, there was a small citizen group that was unhappy about consolidation. They had invested time in the consolidation issue and had been part of the conversation. According to Scott Cockrum, "They were part of many consolidation efforts or inserted themselves in the process to be a distractor of the process or to prevent it." The fact that the proposed RFA would create an additional taxing authority for the City of Lynnwood also caused some citizen concern. No one wanted to pay more taxes.

Scott Cockrum recalls working on the consolidation for about a year. "We were moving in two or three directions at the same time. I wanted to be prepared for any of the possibilities that we completed the RFA, remained a city fire department, or became a contract city to FD1."

Cockrum recognized he had a labor shortage, so he went to Mayor Smith and asked for help. She, in turn, immediately identified a handful of people to help him. It took a team to support Scott Cockrum's efforts to consolidate the Lynnwood Fire Department and Snohomish Fire District One. Cockrum said, "The mayor's approach was relationship building, to trust (but verify), wanting to do what was most right, even when it was uncomfortable, and to give trusted people authority to complete their mission."

Sarah Olson, the deputy director of Lynnwood Parks, Recreation & Cultural Arts Department, eventually ended up being the lead negotiator in the planning. Olson cites Mayor Smith as having made some strategic moves by bringing in Scott Cockrum because he had experience with numerous consolidation efforts. "Since Scott Cockrum had experience with regional fire authority consolidations, Mayor Smith directed us, Chief Cockrum and City administrators/departments, to exit all previous regional planning agreements, so we could deal with only the two agencies: the Lynnwood Fire Department and Fire District One," Olson said.

Chief Cockrum and the team worked through a lot of communication and education and also worked with city leadership. People were aware of what the team was doing and why the consolidation needed to happen. Cockrum said, "In the end, we put everyone—city employees, council and management—in the position of understanding the situation. We gave them all of the facts so they could reach a decision to move the Fire Department from the city's budget.

By the time the consolidation was finalized, Scott Cockrum had moved on and retired from public service. He acknowledges that the decision to become fire chief in Lynnwood was because he wanted to run a small fire department that would require him to have an influence on day-to-day operations and to be out in the public to educate the community. He had also been looking forward to having more influence on the men and women he worked there. He envisioned himself being an advocate for them.

"The consolidation was terrible for me. That's not what I wanted to do." And yet he knew it was the right thing to do. "In the end, once we made the decision to consolidate, I knew it was the right decision—this was the right thing for the Public Safety in that region."

Mayor Smith stated, "Chief Cockrum was appointed by me and confirmed by the council in October 2014. My understanding was that the city had tried to do an RFA since 1972. Scott Cockrum took something that people had been trying to do for 40 years and made it happen in eight months." Sarah Olson, though, cites Mayor Smith as the real leader in the consolidation because she picked the right people to become involved and staked her whole political career on that decision. The vote to consolidate was extremely contentious, so much so that Mayor Smith cast the tie-breaking vote to move forward. She said, "I was determined to set the city and fire district up for success. Chief Cockrum was the right guy at the right time with the right experience. My biggest challenge was making sure he had the resources and emotional energy to get us to the finish line. And we did it!"

In the end, the RFA merger made a difference. Sonja Springer said, "It was fantastic to get those costs (for the Lynnwood Fire Department) off the city's books. Fire departments are expensive. By consolidating with the RFA, it saved the city a significant sum of increased costs. This was a huge win for city finances."

More than saving the city or taxpayers money, major efficiencies also came out of the consolidation. The community would get better service because there are no redundancies between two fire departments—that's a pivotal change for the city that will have lasting benefits forever.

The people of the City of Lynnwood care about many issues but the No. 1 issue the community cares about is safety. When Mayor Smith came into office, she wanted the police department to become more community-focused, to develop a community mindset. This was around the same time that President Barack Obama issued an Executive Order appointing an eleven-member task force on 21st Century Policing to respond to a number of serious incidents between law enforcement and the communities they serve and protect.

The previous chief of police, Steven Jensen was often perceived as being more authoritarian and had a rank-and-file, law-and-order type of leadership style. He was known to be hyperfocused on crime.

"As in any organizational culture, change starts at the top," Mayor Smith commented. "Chief Jensen served as our Lynnwood Chief for 21 years, coming to us from the Oakland Police Department, where he served for 24 years. He was highly respected by the city, region and nationally because of his decades of police experience, but nationally policing was beginning to shift to a community-based policing model. My biggest concern was being able to build trust with him and Lynnwood Police Dept. (LPD) before we could even start to talk about how our police department could move toward a Community Policing model."

Corbitt Loch remembers the challenge he faced when he was assigned to facilitate efficiency studies. In general, departments are not eager to have their internal processes examined by an outside entity. For example, one task was studying the Lynnwood Police Department, which as it turns out, had great results. A short time after the efficiency study was released, the chief and deputy chief decided to retire. They had been there for 20 years and had created a culture. All command staff had been there for 20 years and also had the same mindset.

"Chief Jensen helped to lay the foundation for LPD to begin the fundamental shift toward a Community Policing model," Mayor Smith said, "But in 2016 he decided it was his time to retire. This gave us the opportunity to bring in Chief Tom Davis to spearhead our efforts to build meaningful and trusting relationships with our community, focusing our efforts on community safety and crime prevention."

Chief Steven Jensen's retirement send-off was held in a room packed with his friends, family and colleagues from numerous departments, who all wished him the best but were sorry to see him leave the LPD. While the city worked to find a permanent chief, in the interim, Deputy Chief Bryan Stanifer served as acting chief of police.

Stanifer remembers Mayor Smith as being very supportive of the police department. He described her as being "the epitome of a servant-leader." One of the first things Bryan Stanifer mentions is Snopac, which was the 911 call center that served north Snohomish County. There were two 911 call centers at the time serving all of Snohomish County, one in the north and the other serving the south. The way Stanifer describes it, "The demarcation between north and south was at 128th, creating a no man's land. 911 Calls would go inadvertently to the north or conversely to the south center, then they would have to transfer the call to the appropriate center. Snopac.

"A few extra seconds to transfer a call doesn't sound like a big deal," said Stanifer, "but when a person is in a life-threatening situation, a few seconds can be forever." The two centers were merged, but in order to do so, Mayor Smith worked with other elected officials of the smaller cities such as Brier and Woodway, who wanted the merger to occur as much as the larger cities of Everett or Snohomish.

Stanifer said, "That is a forte of hers, to work with other elected officials. She was able to find common goals and able to see the bigger vision. This is also the case when we were looking at building the new Community Justice Center."

The Lynnwood Police Department underwent a cultural transition from being hyperfocused on law & order (arresting criminals) to becoming a community team player that searches for ways to help all of the people of Lynnwood. One of the key factors that led to this change was recruiting Tom Davis. Davis had been in law enforcement for 30 years. He had spent the majority of that time with the Snohomish County Sheriff's office.

Initially, Davis was only going to be there for six months, to lead the department through an assessment. The city had brought in an outside consulting firm to do a cultural assessment. Davis had planned to leave after the assessment was completed.

"I believed in what we were doing," Davis said. "The mayor believed in me, in what we were doing. We both believed there was a lot of great work to do together. So, I started deciding that I would be there longer." Tom Davis had been in the business of policing for his entire adult life. "Over the years, we develop our own ideas about what the ideal environment would look like," he said. "I had an idea about what I thought community relationships and what policing should be."

Although Mayor Smith's ideas about community policing were from the lens or perspective of a mayor, Tom Davis had similar ideas. After spending about four or five months interacting with the department, Mayor Smith asked Davis what he thought. "I told her she had a police department full of amazing men and women. They just need the opportunity to be amazing. They needed a tone and tenor to support them. The organization needed someone to support the men and women there."

Tom Davis became the chief of police in August 2016. "I began to appreciate the department," he said. "I believed I could provide the road map. I believed what the mayor wanted to accomplish."

"When Tom Davis came on board, it was a great springboard—hey, this is state-of-the-art thinking—Under Mayor Smith's leadership the culture was modified," Corbitt Loch said. "The change in culture would not have happened without her leadership."

The Lynnwood Police Department had always been good at law and order—the traditional model of policing. As a matter of fact, there has always been a bit of controversy over the red-light-traffic-cameras. "The traffic cameras have always been and will always be a hotly debated issue in communities," Davis said. "People ask: 'Is it a traffic safety program or a revenue generator?'"

Davis wasn't in the LPD when the issue of red-light-traffic-cameras was hotly debated and fodder for lawsuits, but he said, "They are in fact a traffic safety tool. Whether people like the cameras or not, they do have a sense of awareness of them while driving in the city." On any given day, 80,000 people travel through Lynnwood. Studies have shown that 80% of the people fined for running red lights do not live in Lynnwood. Studies have also shown that because of the red-light-traffic-cameras, there are fewer accidents. The red-light-traffic-cameras do generate revenue that is used for important programs in the community. People do slow down and don't try to run red lights—and that is a safety issue. There are multiple benefits to the program. The red-light-traffic-cameras are driving both behavior and revenue.

Former City Council Member Rev. M. Christopher Boyer noted that Mayor Smith refined the Red-Light-Camera Project with the police department. There was consistent messaging about how the red-light-cameras have made the roads safer.

"This is really for our good," he said. "Initially, there had been hoopla and litigation over the red-light-cameras, but it's much less of an issue than it was four years ago, which can be attributed to ongoing education and communication."

The new community policing mandate did not steer away from the traditional function to combat crime. Instead, the LPD expanded its message to focus on the needs of a community that wanted to live in a safe environment but also wanted to create a city that was both welcoming and livable. The LPD looked for non-crisis collaboration with the community—because that is where relationships were built.

Two programs, Cops and Clergy and Cops and Kids, gave the police opportunities to connect with the community.

Davis said, "We also began communicating with our diverse communities, our faith-based communities, our Muslim communities. We were essentially doing social work in the community."

At the same time, the members of the LPD did not forget their core missions of holding people accountable, of thinking of themselves as guardians and remaining vigilant. "We are giving our community a sense of feeling safe and protected by the Lynnwood Police Department—that is what Mayor Smith wanted for her community as well," Davis said.

Tom Davis served as chief of police from August 2016 to August 2020. Since August 1, 2020, **Jim Nelson** has been chief of police. He has been with LPD for 27 1/2 years and once served as deputy chief. Under Chief Nelson, the Lynnwood Police Department continues as a superb example of a community-policing model. Chief Nelson places emphasis on opening the doors to look at how the police communicate with the public. He thinks it's essential to put things in more community-minded communication and to move away from the *police-speak*. "We talk a lot about servant leadership," Nelson said. We dedicate a lot of effort to being a superb model. We serve the community in the way they want to be served."

Chief Nelson is aware that the expectations of how a community wants to be served can vary. There is the constant reminder to understand what those expectations are so the police can effectively do their job. Chief Nelson mentioned that there is always something, an incident where we can do better. "There is always work that needs to be done," he said. "The officer who goes to a community event needs to have an empathetic ear, but, at the same time, needs to pursue a suspect who is causing harm."

Being proactive about building community relationships can be held in balance with being vigilant to keep the community safe and holding people who are doing harm accountable. The LPD prides itself on not operating in a vacuum and taking a holistic look at the community. Crime prevention, safety and compassion are not mutually exclusive traits. Keeping Lynnwood safe also means helping to create an environment that is both welcoming and livable. How the mandate of safe, welcoming and livable translates to other social problems facing the city is worth taking a look at.

Chapter 8
Community Health and Safety

Mayor Smith's *servant leadership* style influenced many other facets of the Lynnwood community. She made sure that the governance was in place to ensure healthy, positive, and appropriate growth to create a *safe community*. Major social problems needed to be addressed. Homelessness and drug addiction were both widespread and further complicated by inadequate social services. Programs that help people before they're thrown in jail were underfunded. Jail was not the answer for the chronically drug-addicted. The criminal justice system was ill-equipped to deal with repeat offenders and the reality of a revolving door cycle for drug addicts. With the impending expansion of the light rail, there was the possibility of even more homeless people moving to Lynnwood, a daunting concern given that homelessness was already a problem.

According to Mayor Smith, "Bringing social services into south Snohomish County is a focus of mine. Until now, social service programs have been mainly available in north Snohomish County and in Everett."

People living below the poverty line had children in the public school system. In the Edmonds School District, which serves Lynnwood, there were approximately 640 students from homeless families. There were meal programs that sent nutritional food home to students every weekend and throughout the summer months. These programs were not coordinated locally, countywide or through the state. These programs were being funded through private donations.

One nonprofit organization that offered unique social services was the Foundation for Edmonds School District. The foundation develops community partnerships and bridges sustainable funding in support of the Edmonds School District's children, families, and educators in their pursuit of educational excellence.

The foundation's executive director, **Deborah Brandi,** defined their Nourishing Network Program as now being 7 or 8 years old. The Edmonds School District came to the foundation and asked them to develop a solution to make sure that the homeless children are fed.

"If our kids are hungry and their basic needs are not met, they can't learn," Brandi said. The number of children that are fed by the program ebbs and flows. Through the years, the program has expanded from feeding children during the weekdays, to providing meals on the weekends, as well as during the long summer months.

Mayor Smith and Deborah Brandi worked together on a number of initiatives ranging from grassroots initiatives, such as food programs and fundraising events to housing projects. Deborah Brandi and Mayor Smith worked together on summer meals projects. The program is now in its seventh year of delivering summer meals to four locations where families can pick up meals for their children. Another major project involved the Monster Mad Dash, an annual fundraising event held during the first Saturday of each October. For this event, the foundation partnered with both Alderwood Mall and the City of Lynnwood. The question Deborah Brandi always poses is *how do we lift an entire family out of multigenerational poverty*?

Mayor Smith also asked that same question and sought solutions that would help to break the cycle of poverty. As an advocate for the homeless, she was especially known for having a soft spot in her heart for the children. The mayor sought a way to provide transitional housing for homeless children in the school district.

Rodeo Inn, a rundown motel on Highway 99, soon became the Rodeo Inn Project. Termed as a blighted property, the Rodeo Inn was more than run down. For years, the Lynnwood Police Department had been inundated with calls about crime and drug overdoses. As a former hotbed for drugs and prostitution, the motel had been condemned. Mayor Smith saw an opportunity to rehabilitate the property to house homeless kids who needed shelter so they could attend school.

Deborah Brandi remembers that the Rodeo Inn became a collaborative effort. **Robin Fenn,** who at the time was CEO of Verdant Health Commission, also became involved with the Rodeo Inn Project. As part of the program of Public Hospital District No. 2, Snohomish County, the Verdant Health Commission works to provide support and opportunities for people to improve their health and well-being. Verdant serves nearly 200,000 in Brier, Edmonds, Lynnwood, Mountlake Terrace, Woodway and in portions of Bothell and unincorporated Snohomish County. Verdant provides funding for a wide range of health services.

Aside from being CEO of the Verdant Health Commission, Robin Fenn was part of a CEO Roundtable in south Snohomish County. The group included the city manager for Mountlake Terrace, the Mayor of Edmonds, other local politicians and influencers. It was a closed group that met once a quarter and a great venue for people to support one another and work together. Robin Fenn said, "We didn't want it to be a formal group with minutes or documentation." For a school district, a public hospital, a foundation and the city, to work together was the height of innovative collaboration. Under Mayor Smith's leadership, the group started looking at the Rodeo Inn.

Deborah Brandi remembers that the first property did not pass inspection. "It was so contaminated from drug use that it would have cost too much to bring it up to become a serviceable property." The Rodeo Inn itself was abandoned as a potential site for transitional housing. The good news was that a solid collaboration had been formed and its participants continued to search for the right property. "Going forward, the foundation will be involved on a deeper level and this will strengthen our community partnerships," Brandi said. "There is a better building that can be turned into transitional housing." Brandi mentioned moving forward with a parcel of property owned by the Edmonds School District that will be transformed into housing for the homeless children and their families in the district. And while technically it is a different property, the idea originated with Mayor Smith and the Rodeo Inn.

Other key influencers in Snohomish County played a key role in Mayor Smith's initiative to provide transitional housing for the homeless. Stephanie Wright was a past member of the Lynnwood City Council and is currently on the Snohomish County Council. Stephanie Wright backed Mayor Smith on the Rodeo Inn project for affordable housing, and while this particular property did not come to fruition, Stephanie Wright thinks the collaborative effort made on the project showed what could be done.

"We were making something happen," Wright said. "The conversations with Verdant and the Edmonds School District show the collaboration needed to create housing for homeless families of the school district. The families could be quantified, and a solution could be identified—and this could be explained to the community. Those are the best parts about being in government."

The project was never short-circuited for any other reason than the building could not be renovated. The Rodeo Inn was sold, remediated and cleaned. No longer a hotbed for crime, the Rodeo Inn is now a thriving business under new ownership.

In addition to homelessness and drug addiction, there were other issues looming on the horizon: mental illness, racism, and the assimilation of the growing immigrant population into the community. The state mental health hospitals were not meeting the needs of the mentally ill. Emergency rooms were bursting at the seams. At one point, a 16-bed detox center recently opened in an industrial district that was supported by Catholic Community Services and the Verdant Hospital District. And even though it was in an industrial district, there were people who were opposed to the facility and did not want it in their own backyards

Even before the Black Lives Matter movement and the high-profile national attention given to police shootings, the Lynnwood community was concerned for its safety and security. There was a sense of danger people felt due to the changing demographics in the Lynnwood community. The ugly side of racism had been uncovered nationally as well and that had an impact on the Lynnwood community. People were being more guarded in their actions. There was the perception that people who are from diverse communities do not have to be treated in a civil manner. And this made people who are marginalized feel threatened. There was also a perception problem with undocumented immigrants—children were afraid their parents were going to be deported.

Along with opioid abuse, or drug addiction in general, came an increase in crime, especially thefts and burglaries. Businesses were in jeopardy. Addicts stole from stores. Many Lynnwood residents felt threatened by the addicts. In Lynnwood, there were sections of town that had blight houses, old houses abandoned due to bank foreclosures. When the bank forecloses on a house and boards it up, then the homeless and addicts squat in these abandoned homes.

Code enforcement time was spent dealing with blight homes that had squatters because it was a public health hazard. Law enforcement could get squatters to vacate, but it was only temporary. Drug addicts came back, leaving needles, garbage and very unsanitary conditions, especially because the utilities had been turned off, so the water was not running and sewer lines backed up. For the community, the addiction problem coupled with blight homes was very disruptive and scary. At one point, Dr. Gary Goldbaum, health officer for the Snohomish Health District said, "Snohomish County is sort of at the epicenter of the opioid problem in Washington state."

Prior to the changing culture of the Lynnwood Police Department, there had been real tension between the police and the community. The changing dynamics of the Lynnwood Police Department made it possible for it to become a superb example of community policing. Former Lynnwood Police Chief Tom Davis said, "Today there is a big conversation about whether policing should be social work. The police department does have a role because we are the first responders in crisis situations working with homelessness and mental health challenges."

The Lynnwood Police Department hired an in-house professional social worker and created a team to do outreach for those struggling with addiction, homelessness and mental health issues. "We need to equip the police department because they respond to people in crisis," Davis said.

There was a critical need to fund human social services and a detox center. Drug addiction, homelessness, and mental health issues were three different problems that could be interrelated, but, on the other hand, they might not be connected to one another. Mayor Smith acknowledged the complexity of these health and safety issues and that there was no one-size-fits-all solution. These urgent needs paved the way for several pragmatic solutions.

The first project aimed to build the City of Lynnwood Community Justice Center. The new center will house the police department, a reimagined misdemeanor jail that includes social service support, and a remodeled court, which will allow the necessary space and function to bring the best justice services to the community.

Former Police Chief Davis said, "I'm incredibly excited for the building to come to fruition, not just as a structure. It is the embodiment of the philosophy that Nicola and I have about how the community can benefit from services and we can come together with the community." The new Community Justice Center is the reality of the police department and social services coming together to benefit the community. "That is the way policing should be done," Davis added. "We're out front on that. I'm really happy for the city."

Mayor Smith, along with Verdant CEO Robin Fenn, also reached out to the Community Health Center of Snohomish County. The Community Health Center of Snohomish County (CHC) is a nonprofit provider that serves the health needs of county residents who face barriers, usually financial, to health care. The CHC offers primary medical and dental services. The CHC practices patient-centered care, where a team of health care professionals works with an individual to build an ongoing relationship based on the individual's health care needs. Mayor Smith established this unique collaboration and partnership with the Community Health Center of Snohomish County to bring services and options to the Lynnwood community. The collaboration also focuses on addressing and reducing the underlying causes of recidivism, to deal with repeat offenders and the reality of the revolving door cycle for drug addicts.

Chief of Police Jim Nelson commented, "Certainly in the past people (in crisis) would have been charged with crimes. This is a compassionate solution. We can't have a one-size-fits-all approach. We have a multipronged approach. There is enforcement—getting people through the Community Health Center, where there is the continuity of care."

Another collaborative project, the Law Enforcement Assisted Diversion program (LEAD) offered an alternative to incarceration. The Lynnwood Police Department partnered with the Snohomish County Prosecutor's Office and the Everett Police Department on LEAD. This grant- funded pilot program aims to keep people in crisis, out of jail, and gives officers alternatives to arrest. Instead, people in crisis are offered drug treatment and mental health counseling services and ongoing support—the opportunity to ultimately kick drug dependency. **Police Chief Nelson said,** "We are very fortunate to have an engaged community, working for a good organization in a good city."

All three of these projects offered innovative solutions to drug addiction, homelessness and mental illness, and while there was no quick fix, it was the beginning of a solution moving forward in the right direction. The irony is that one day, these systemic solutions would have a profound and lasting impact on Mayor Smith's own personal life.

Robin Fenn, past CEO of Verdant Health Commission, worked with Mayor Smith on a wide range of projects. Together with Lynn Sordel, the director of the Parks and Recreation Department, and Mayor Smith, Robin Fenn became part of a team. The team did a survey to determine what social services were needed and put it out to the whole Lynnwood community. They were able to identify what was needed the most. Affordable housing, access to health care, and mental health treatment were among the top needs. There was a focus on different ethnic groups and diversity. They also determined what was working and what was not working. The outgrowth of that work led Mayor Smith to spend a lot of time working on the initiatives that would drive real solutions.

Working on homelessness was not a new area of focus for Mayor Smith. When she was an administrator at Edmonds College, she worked on a number of initiatives to help homeless students. Cassie Franklin, Mayor of Everett, remembers being impressed with Mayor Smith during those days when she was with Edmonds College. "She is a compassionate leader," Mayor Franklin said. "It's great to have a like-minded leader with heart and passion and a focus on equity. She is doing the right things for the right reasons for her community." Through the years, Mayor Franklin and Mayor Smith served on a number of boards related to homelessness and worked on solutions to homelessness. "Mayor Smith is very compassionate about these complex issues, but she is pragmatic as well," said Mayor Cassie Franklin.

Protecting the community to create genuine Public Safety is like conducting an orchestra and requires a coordination of effort. Mayor Smith facilitated the creation of the **Community Health and Safety Section**—which had five city departments working in tandem. The Community Health and Safety Section led by the police department, became a force for interdepartmental collaboration among the Fire Marshal, Police, Public Works, Parks and Community Development to work together as a coalition. The Community Health and Safety Section also brings safety resources into the high schools.

The city formed a contract with the YWCA and one person who works with the homeless population to help them find services and housing. The contract between the city and the YWCA was the final product of the city council's Taskforce on Homelessness that had been initiated and chaired by Rev. M. Christopher Boyer. "It was the first time, insofar as anyone I've talked to was aware that Lynnwood had ever spent money specifically on social services," Boyer said. The contract led to the creation of the city's Human Services Commission and their grants program made available to social service agencies. They have since added a social worker and another police officer.

According to Mayor Smith, "The mission of the Community Health and Safety Section is to leverage community partnerships;

institute creative problem-solving techniques through a unified interdepartmental approach, and foster outreach through education to address conditions that fuel crime and public disorder while maintaining a proactive stance on criminal trends and nuisance problems that impact the quality of life for citizens in Lynnwood."

Public Safety encompasses more than physical safety but also has emotional ramifications. The elements of nurturing a community and of building trust are equally important. Community trust, the trust that a community has in its leadership, is hard to earn and takes time to earn but can be lost in an instant. Robin Fenn said, "With other politicians, they have one or two key agenda items and the rest fall to the side. With Nicola, she has kept many balls in the air because her mission was always to ask: *What is best for the residents of this city?*"

2009: Rotarian Group Study trip to India with Dena, Wendy, Faimous, Kyle, Nicola, and Warren.

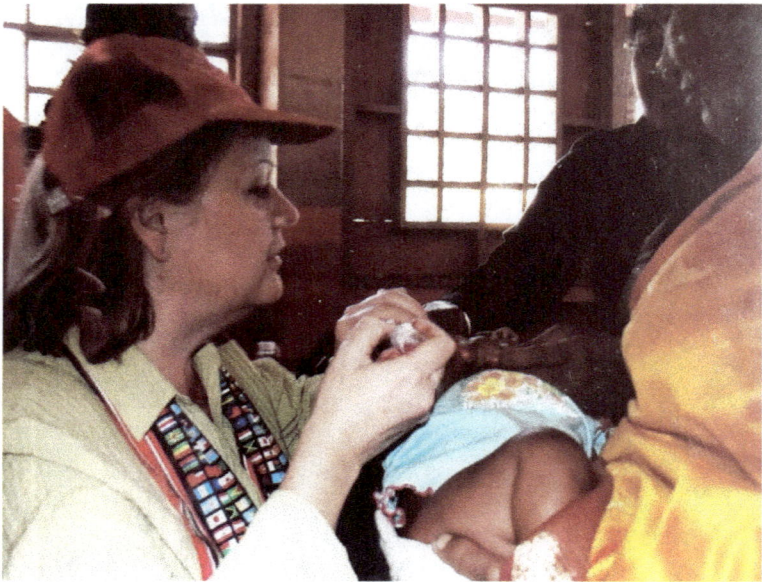

2009: Nicola administers polio drops to children in India.

2012 Rotarian Community Service Project with Andrew Ballard, Jeffery Goodwin, Nicola, Jon Neimi, Sandra Ballard.

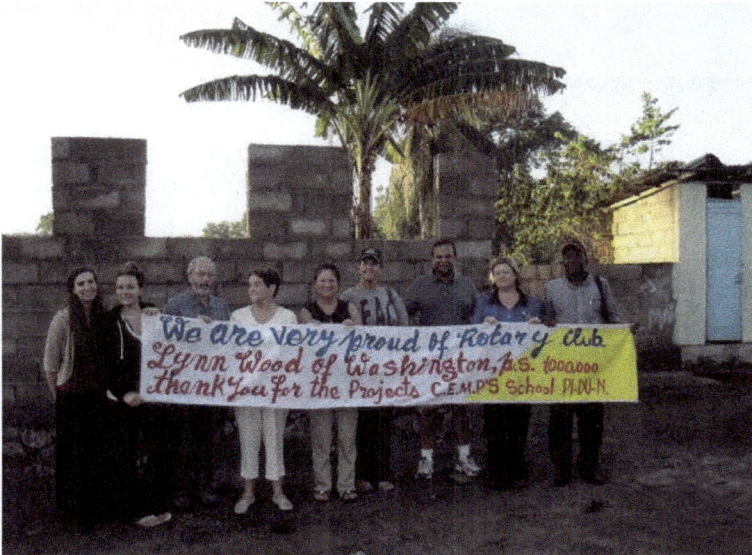

2013: Rotarian Humanitarian trip to Haiti.

2013: With Gunnvor Tveidt and Theresa Poalucci on the campaign trail.

2013: The results are in! Nicola Smith is the next Mayor of Lynnwood.

2014: "Strong Mayor" with Ki Seung Cho (AKA Master Cho) at a local Tae Kwon Do Competition.

2015: National Night Out event with Lynnwood Fire Chief Scott Cockrum (retired).

2015: Rabbi Berel Paltiel and family during the Menorah Lighting Celebration hosted at City Hall.

2015: Community Transit Swift Blue Line Ribbon Cutting with Emmett Heath and Jean Hernandez.

2016: The First State of the City Address at the Lynnwood Convention Center.

2016: Promotional Ceremony for then Deputy Chief James Nelson with Deputy Chief Bryan Stanifer (retired) and Chief of Police Steve Jensen (retired).

2018: Nicola with Lynnwood Police Department's honorary "Little Chief" Luca.

2016: Bike2Health Ribbon Cutting with Parks Deputy Director Sarah Olson, Parks Director Lynn Sordel, Mayor Dave Earling, Verdant Health Commissioner Deana Knutsen, and City Engineer David Mach.

2016: Official Sister City Ceremony with Mayor Choi of Damyang, South Korea and Snohomish County Executive Dave Somers.

2016: Nicola and the Lynnwood City Council at a Veterans Day event at Veterans Park, committed to making Lynnwood a veteran-supportive city.

2017: Grand opening of the Veterans Heritage Museum with founders Zabine Van Ness and Todd Crooks.

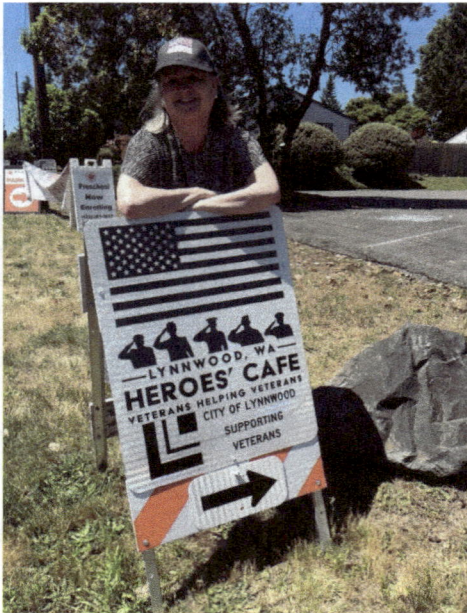

Mayor Smith pointing the way to the Heroes' Café.

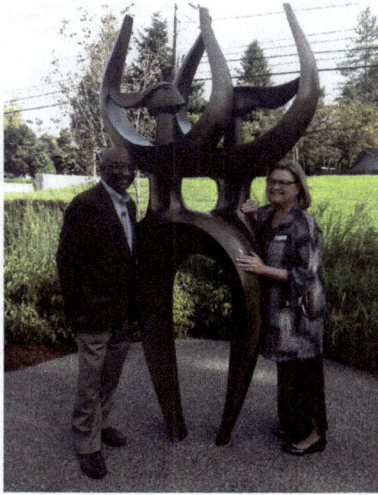

2016: With long-time friend and campaign
manager Wally Webster.

2016: With Strategic Planner Corbitt Loch, IT
Director Will Cena at Leadership Snohomish County.

2017: Mayor's Team: Leah Jensen, Art Ceniza, Nicola Smith, Gina Israel, and Julie Moore.

2017: After reelection, swearing In ceremony with Judge Stephen Moore.

After 2021: With Frantz Joycelyn Donat.

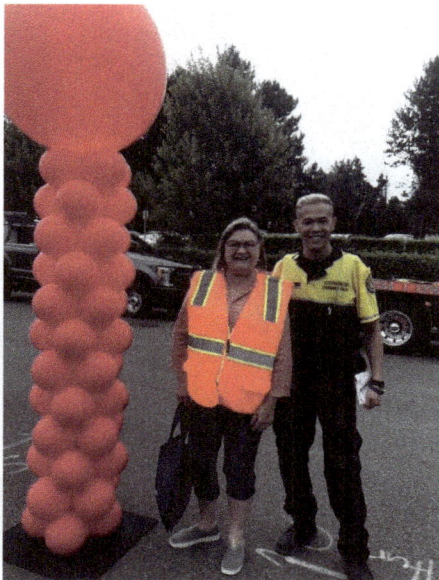

2018: With Lynnwood business owner Phong Nguyen
at the Fair on 44th event.

2017: Washington D.C. With Washington Senator Patty Murray to advocate for transportation funding, Public Works Director Bill Franz and City Engineer David Mach.

2017: Washington D.C. With Washington Senator Maria Cantwell, And representatives from the Economic Alliance of Snohomish County.

2017: Washington, D.C. With US Congressmen Rick Larsen.

2017: Olympia - With Senator Marko Liias and Art Ceniza during City Action Days.

2018: Women Mayors – With Kyoko Matsumoto-Wright (Mountlake Terrace), Jenny Durkan (Seattle), Jennifer Gregerson (Mukilteo), Cassie Franklin (Everett).

2018: Maple Road Project: Council Member Christine Frizzell, Mayor Smith, and County Council Member Stephanie Wright. County.

2018: With Diversity, Equity & Inclusion Commissioner Naz Lashgari celebrating the Persian New Year (Nowruz).

2020: With social activist Joshua Binda during a Black Lives Matter rally at Lynnwood City Hall.

2019: Sound Transit Lynnwood Link Extension Ground Breaking Ceremony for the Lynnwood City Center Station.

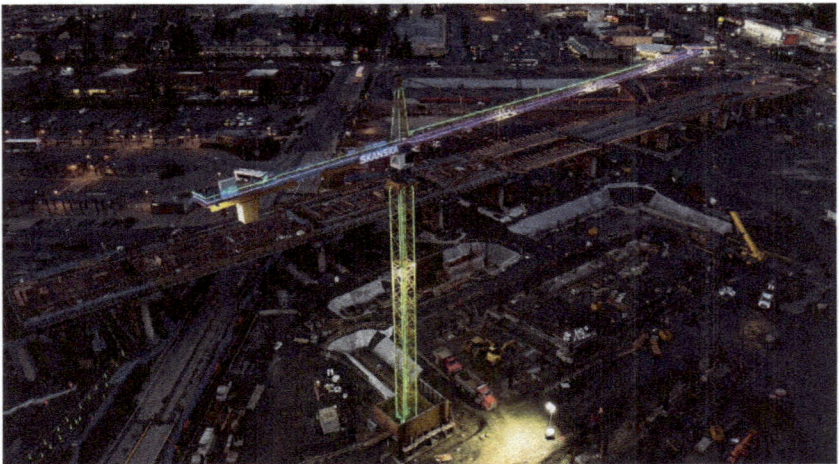

2021: Construction crane at the site of the Sound Transit Lynnwood City Center Station.

2020: Rendering of the future Community Justice Center.

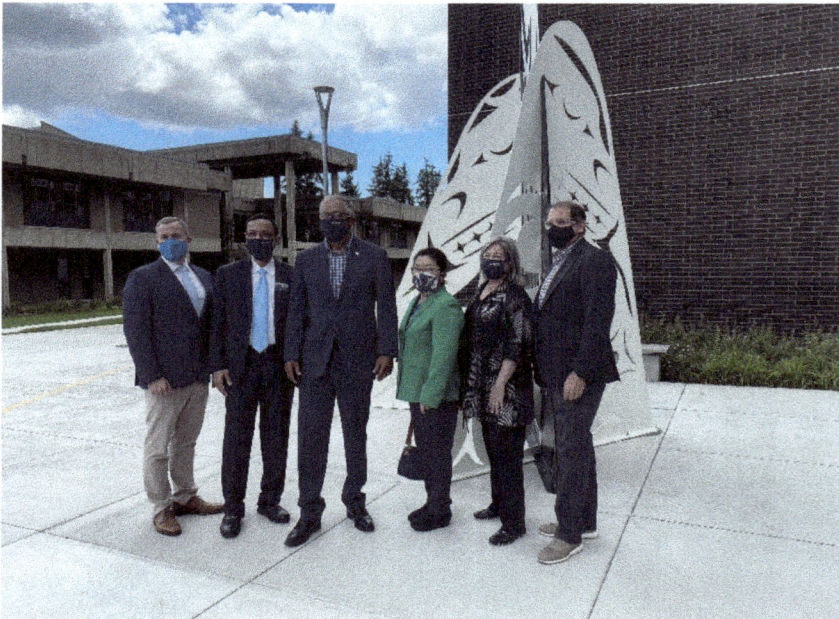

2021: Tour of the STEM Building at Edmonds College with Governor Jay Inslee, Mayor Mike Nelson (Edmonds), Edmonds College President Amit Singh, Washington Representatives Cindy Ryu, and Strom Peterson.

2020: First COVID-19 Snohomish County Mayor's Press Conference, With Mayor Cassie Franklin (Everett) and Mayor Jon Nehring (Marysville).

2021: Ground breaking ceremony of the South Lynnwood Park Renovation Project.

2020: Unveiling the new *All Are Welcome* signal box wrap in the Alderwood Mall area.

Warm and welcoming Executive Office at City Hall, *Stand of Trees* painting by Theresa Poalucci.

2017: Re-Election Night, Backrow - Ben (nephew), Del (husband), Nicola, Emily (daughter), Greg (son-in-law). Front row – Kendall (granddaughter), Tia (daughter), and Julian (grandson).

Front row- Emily holding Skylar, Julian, Nicola, Kendall, Tia holding Elijah Back row standing- Greg, Del, Dylan

Chapter 9
Lynnwood is Open for Business

A city is responsible for creating an environment that supports a healthy economy by meeting the needs of its business owners and business leaders. Yet economic and business growth had been stalled in Lynnwood for many years. David Kleitsch came to Lynnwood in 2001 and has been with the city through four mayors and 10 city councils. He is now the longest-serving department head. "I've seen many people in and out, and come and go," he said. Initially, he was hired to establish the Department of Economic Development. "Until then, Lynnwood had never had that position before," he said. "A Community Vision Plan was created in 2008 but never implemented. The city did not know how to make it happen."

n 2008 there was a totally unsettled political environment. The city's politics had been historically confrontational. The mayor and the city council fought, and staff was caught between the two. "We had an election to abolish the mayor's position and go to a city manager position," Kleitsch said. "It was really fractured, and we were stuck. Not only were we stuck, we were split into silos. How miserable the political situation was!"

From the onset, Mayor Smith was aware that organizational changes among the city's departments and personnel needed to be made. She encouraged open communication and autonomy among all of the city's staff. She also made it clear that anyone could come to her office to talk to the mayor. The open-door policy that she offered to her staff was expanded to the public. Every Wednesday afternoon was reserved so that anyone in the community could meet with her.

The city had been working on changing the business application process since 2015. Due to Mayor Smith's commitment to Rotary and other civic organizations, she had heard about the complicated permitting process. Meeting with business members of the community during her open Wednesday meetings gave her even more information. "We need to do better," she remarked. "A positive business climate is essential to achieving strong economic growth, and a customer-centric approach will provide a supportive business climate that makes doing business in Lynnwood attractive and a positive experience."

Phong Nguyen remembers reaching out to the mayor around 2017. Before meeting with Mayor Smith, he did his homework. Governor Jay Inslee had signed a memorandum, the Cascadia Innovation Memorandum of Understanding, confirming the mutual interests of both the Seattle area and Vancouver, BC—they wanted to create regional economic opportunities for innovation and technology along the I-5 corridor from Seattle to Vancouver, BC.

Phong put together a presentation about the Governor's Cascadia Innovation Memorandum of Understanding, or MOU, and invited other members of the business community. The intent of the meeting was for Phong to introduce himself. "My goal was to provide a partnership with the city, helping to bring technology and innovation to the city in the coming years," Phong said. "I knew growth was going to happen in Lynnwood. I knew something big was going to happen here. And there would be a lot of challenges to come along with that growth, especially with permitting."

Phong also noted that the Lynnwood business community was going through tough times. Along the retail corridor, businesses were closing their doors. The city had lost several furniture stores in a few years and he did not understand why. He invited the mayor to visit his store to further the conversation. Mayor Smith brought the city's economic development director, David Kleitsch, to the meeting. "We had a great conversation," Phong said.

Soon after Phong was invited by the mayor and David Kleitsch to attend the city council meetings and to become more informed about what the council was doing to help the business climate. Phong remembers being the only business owner in the council chambers. He thought there was a huge disconnect between the city and the business community. He then created the Lynnwood

Business Consortium—composed of business owners, residents, developers and builders. Again, he met with Mayor Smith along with city council member Shannon Sessions, Shanon Tysland, owner of Experience Momentum, and Linda Jones, president/CEO Lynnwood Chamber of Commerce.

According to Phong, they recommended that he should join the Lynnwood Chamber of Commerce and work closely with Linda Jones to help with the city's economic development. At the time the chamber was brand-new. "Linda and I formed a great relationship," Phong said. Moving forward, several other meetings took place in the city council chambers. "It woke up the city to see there are people who are really passionate about the problems here." According to Phong, *the city had a reputation of, "It's my way or the highway."*

There were many small businesses and restaurants, but the city's reputation was terrible. Developers didn't want to build in Lynnwood. Then came the shake-up. "It took several years to change," Julie Moore said. "Not an easy fix. It required ripping apart the process and making a culture change. We're just now getting on the downward slope to having all of the fixes made."

Changing the city's work culture meant getting staff to shift their perspective from stonewalling to wanting to help people. Corbitt Loch noted, "Governments don't have to make changes in how they do things. They do not operate in a competitive environment. When businesses behave this way, they are in danger of going out of business. Businesses have to make changes based on market demand and competition."

Companies like Montgomery Ward, Radio Shack, Eastman Kodak and Sears, just to name a few, were resistant to change and went out of business. This is not true of the government. There is no market competition in government. Mayor Smith's challenge was to accomplish the changes and she accomplished the change, but it wasn't done overnight.

David Kleitsch said, "Government isn't like business. The CEO can fire everyone and set up the culture they want because the fixed goal is profit. It's a little different in the public sector."

Wally Webster, who was the campaign manager of Mayor Smith's reelection campaign (*Maintain the Momentum*) in 2017 recalled that it took longer to move people out who needed to be moved out. As a result, it was questioned whether she was the right person for the job. "Over time that changed and that's why she was reelected," he said. "Developers and businesspeople were turned off by the delays and incompetence of the city's business permits departments." Webster attributes the fact that it took longer for her to move people out because she "leaned too far to the human side."

Removing long-term employees is complicated and often has legal ramifications. "She moved us more into a customer service culture," David Kleitsch said. "The customer is not the enemy. It's OK to work with them. We can change our processes. Just because we always did it a certain way doesn't mean we will always have to do it that way. "She was good at embracing and advancing the vision, and people could see we were serious about it, and in that process, she became a touchstone for the city."

The mayor and the city council worked together to create greater efficiencies. They looked at community development, specifically planning, and how it interacted across various disciplines. Four departments, the Fire Marshall, the Community Development Department, the Economic Development Department, and various Public Works responsibilities related to private development, now became housed under a single entity—giving birth to Development and Business Services (DBS). The reorganized departments were still independent but working together in the same building. In order to create efficiency with a focus on customer service, questions were asked: How do we serve our customers? How do we work together? How do we embrace the community? How do we fix what's broken? Through all of that effort, Mayor Smith created a far superior climate for the business community. "They got it done and it's working extremely well," Wally Webster said.

Mayor Smith recalls that changing the internal mindset to become customer-focused wasn't an easy task. Some employees were unwilling to be part of the sweeping changes being made.

There was resistance to going forward in a new direction. David Kleitsch now oversees DBS. He knows all of the history and has been a change agent to make this major transition. This systemic long-term change was needed and will continue to manifest itself forever in many different ways—a huge benefit to the community.

Word quickly spread to the business owners. Phong Nguyen said, "A builder told me that a number of city inspectors suddenly left. Some left to work for other cities. Some retired early. Some were fired. Community Development Director Paul Kraus retired. The head building official resigned. A lot of the inspectors did not like Mayor Smith's customer-centric approach to things. She went in and cleaned up shop." Real estate developer Jeff Butler was delighted by the changes made. "There were developers and investors who refused to go to Lynnwood and now they all come here. There is a different attitude in Lynnwood now."

The creation of Development and Business Services (DBS) made it possible for business owners to do the permitting process online. "Mayor Smith brought in the right people who understand innovation," Butler said. "By the time I finished the Triton Court (Student Housing), one of the builders said, 'that is one of the easiest projects we have ever had.'" The changes made it easier for entrepreneurs to do business in Lynnwood. "I'm hearing from businesspeople that the permitting process is now such a pleasant experience, Phong Nguyen said.

To promote economic development, someone has to champion that. While growth is inevitable, it also needs to be managed. It was Mayor Smith's mission to grow Lynnwood into a city where growth has been managed responsibly. "We are fully committed to creating an environment of operational and organizational excellence," she said. "Part of that includes examining our processes and the culture of how we do business." She participated in many business roundtable discussions, part of bringing people together to focus on finding solutions. Culturally speaking, she changed the city's way of thinking. City Administrator Art Ceniza said, "There have been significant reorganizations at the City of Lynnwood to promote economic sustainability."

In Mayor Smith's vision for the city, economic development encompassed the formation of both large and small businesses. It wasn't only about creating a friendly environment for the big box stores in the vicinity of *Alderwood* (formerly referred to as Alderwood Mall). For example, she supported the expansion of Alderwood to include new dining and retail establishments, and multifamily housing. Yet she also welcomed the mom-and-pop shops, entrepreneurs and technology startups.

The city created an Economic Development Action Plan that called for diversification of the city's economic base and identified opportunities to grow mixed-use centers and to accommodate new retail trends. Mayor Smith gave her support to current businesses by forming relationships with the Snohomish County Economic Alliance and the Lynnwood Chamber of Commerce. Both organizations championed the interests of a diverse range of businesspeople.

David Kleitsch said, "While she supports the big things like Sound Transit and economic development at Alderwood, she's big on nurturing the community. The moms and pops—people who want to work with the city but don't know how."

Linda Jones, president/CEO of the Lynnwood Chamber of Commerce, remembers meeting Mayor Smith for the first time at a ribbon-cutting ceremony.

"She understands the importance of successful business in her city. She understands partnerships and the whole economic cycle and was very good at supporting that." Jones cites the mayor's approachability and how important it is to have the support of the city and the mayor behind her efforts. As a Chamber president, Jones has worked with a number of elected officials.

"It surprised me how many mayors focus on community, businesses and government," she said. "Sometimes mayors focus on one aspect over the other. Mayor Smith understands all areas: community, businesses and government, how they work together and how they support each other."

The elements that need to be in place to support business development include having affordable housing, a skilled workforce and efficient government. "Working with the city is more of a personal experience," Jones said. "She has made every department in the city approachable for businesses and people. You don't feel like a number. They make every effort to do something right. When I call, someone answers the phone."

The city has reached out to the Chamber as a collaborative partner. David Kleitsch's right-hand person stays in touch with Linda Jones. Together they work on business development efforts or focused initiatives to help businesses form and grow. Jones points out that this type of relationship-building is not common in every city. "It seems like that would be the norm, but it's not necessarily that way."

Mayor Smith also recognized the importance of entrepreneurial opportunity and its impact on the local economy. Taking the time and effort to support startups has a profound impact on the community. **Diane Kamionka** is executive director and founder of the NW Innovation Resource Center (NWIRC), an organization that works with entrepreneurs and inventors in Northwest Washington to identify the strategy, tools, and community resources needed to bring their products and business ideas to life. Kamionka acknowledges that the NWIRC helps entrepreneurs to develop effective strategies to start and build a business. Mayor Smith invited Diane Kamionka to join Partner Lynnwood.

Partner Lynnwood meets quarterly and is made up of the Lynnwood Chamber of Commerce, the Edmonds Chamber of Commerce, Edmonds College, the City of Lynnwood, the Sno-Isle Libraries, SCORE, the Small Business Development Center of Washington and Alderwood. All of these different people get together to talk about what initiatives they are working on. **Kathy Coffey, executive director, Leadership Snohomish County, said,** "The intention is to have open communication on a regular basis to create systems or processes that work for everyone." The group usually meets at Edmonds College.

According to David Kleitsch, "Mayor Smith championed Partner Lynnwood with the college and sustained that relationship through two college presidents."

Current Edmonds College President **Amit Singh** said, "Nicola Smith has worked for the college for 27 years—that understanding and that experience is crucial to the partnership between the college and the city." Having had extensive experience of working with both the students and the administration of Edmonds College, Mayor Smith knew that new job opportunities would emerge with the construction of the light rail. Sound Transit had forecast a shortage of 1,700 full-time skilled labor positions. This concern led the mayor to realize we have an opportunity to grow the earning power of our residents while supporting the construction of the public transit system approved by voters. She realized that the college's students could avail themselves of opportunities that began with minimum-wage jobs that would evolve into living-wage, career positions. She worked with Dr. Amit Singh to create a pre-apprenticeship program to attract high school graduates and underemployed individuals and support their entry into construction crafts that might have previously seemed to be out of reach. Dr. Singh said, "She had done a good job of uniting people bringing all stakeholders to the table and finding solutions and moving forward."

Mayor Smith has been supportive of the NW Innovation Resource Center and the development of new businesses: entrepreneurs, inventors and innovators. Diane Kamionka made it clear that the mayor is very accessible and available for insights and advice.

"We do a lot of work with mayors," Kamionka said. "You can tell when you meet political people if they are devout about innovation and startups or not. She was very curious and open and available to talk or meet and to make introductions. She was very impressive." Kamionka cited Mayor Smith as one of the people she trusts and can count on to ask questions, or if she needs direction, and she feels very comfortable asking her to get a direct response. The mayor has also made it clear to her staff that she supports the NWIRC, has made introductions, and invites the group to participate in the annual State of the City event.

Making organizational change is hard. Organizational management experts often describe how it's even more challenging to sustain lasting change. Streamlining the city's business services, some claim, will be Mayor Smith's legacy. Lynnwood's quality of life was directly connected to the community's ability to engage in commerce, i.e., to make a living. Organizational success came from the top down. She made it a priority to turn around the relationships among business, government and the community. She was able to change the thinking of many of the city's employees. She did not have to fire anyone *per se*. Those who did not change their way of thinking left. Now it's very customer-first, as it should be.

Chapter 10
Regional Leadership

Before Mayor Smith came along, Lynnwood was perceived as being an island of one. Mayor Smith changed that. Throughout her career as an administrator and as a public servant, she sought new partnerships and nurtured existing relationships. Equipped with formidable leadership assets, she empowered her staff to do their best work. They felt listened to. They felt like experts and she valued them. By empowering her staff, she took Lynnwood to the next level. The vision for a city center that had long ago been conceived was coming to fruition. More importantly, her own visionary plan defining the five priorities for the city had expanded and became further refined. Lynnwood was on the road to becoming known as a collaborative regional leader. "She supports the county as a whole." Linda Jones said. "She's not running Lynnwood in a bubble. She's active on boards across Snohomish County. She includes other cities. She can see the big picture. She sees how working together makes it better for all of us."

Forming partnerships was a new concept for the City of Lynnwood. Mayor Smith reached out and met every director of government, nonprofit and for-profit entities in the area: colleges, housing groups, other municipalities and other elected officials. She went out of her way and made it a priority to give Lynnwood a presence in a regional community. Many problems that beset a city are often too big to solve alone. More resources are available when partnerships are in place. It just makes good sense to take on partners. "Looking back, it was pretty radical, and it took a while for the region to trust the new Lynnwood," Corbitt Loch said. "It didn't take that long, though, before other entities and organizations thought it was a great change and wanted to work with Lynnwood. For Lynnwood, it was a new day for the community!"

Aside from being a cultural shift for how the city had always done business, there were long-term benefits that no one could have possibly anticipated. Mayor Smith established relationships with state and federal delegations. Lynnwood became a regional model of leadership. Sarah Olson said, "Lynnwood is at the epicenter of a lot of growth and we have been awarded a great number of grants that can only happen when we have a number of things going for us. We have excellent relationships."

The changes made within the city's internal culture had a direct impact on the way the city's top administrators now interacted with other municipalities, elected officials and key stakeholders like Sound Transit and Community Transit.

Former Lynnwood City Council member Sid Roberts said, "Light rail was in gear. She did great work around that. Her greatest accomplishment was completely changing the relational culture of the staff from one of distrust to trust." Roberts asserted that Mayor Smith had changed the city's culture to the extent that people began to do things differently because they had a servant-leader setting an example. "She set the tone for that change," he said. Different people could do the same job, but it was the way she spoke that made a difference. Roberts thought the essence of her skill set was being kind, sympathetic and a really good person. "Nicola created a 180-degree relational change. People felt like they could relax and work together."

Mayor Smith became involved with the Snohomish County Cities Association, which is a large group of elected officials, council members and mayors, who get together monthly to discuss all of the issues impacting them. Kyoko Matsumoto-Wright, the mayor of Mountlake Terrace, cited Lynnwood as an emerging collaborative regional leader due to Mayor Smith's efforts. "She became chair of that organization," Mayor Matsumoto-Wright said. "She was so good at facilitating meetings and keeping everyone from Snohomish County's Cities and Towns focused on the positive."

Mayor Earling recalls Mayor Smith succeeded him as the Snohomish County Cities chairperson. "We collaborated together a great deal. We became 'friends' dealing at the professional level." The group of elected officials from towns and cities in Snohomish County met every month to solve problems and to collaborate together on key pieces of legislation. Mayor Earling found it irritating when leaders at the municipal level tried to stay only at their level without looking at the entire region encompassing the counties of King, Snohomish and Pierce. His collaboration with Mayor Smith looked at the big picture. "We worked on things together and to learn how it figures into the regional thought process and the regional picture."

Mayor Smith formed strong bonds with other mayors. **Jon Nehring,** the mayor of Marysville recalls always having enjoyed the Association of Snohomish County Cities and Towns, but it became more meaningful when Mayor Smith led it. "She took the bull by the horns and made this a group that matters. It was her mission to give it some horsepower," Mayor Nehring said. The group had always been an important part of the social and political fabric of the county, but Mayor Smith seemed bent on making the group stronger and a more dynamic influence in the region. "She is a very collaborative mayor. It's not part of the mayor's job description but shows her willingness to collaborate in ways that benefit all of us."

Mayor Smith often viewed her role as being part of a nationwide, grassroots movement where a new generation of leaders is emerging to create effective change. Instead of bluster and crony tactics, coalitions are formed based on collaboration, mutual respect and the recognition that only a commitment to stewardship will build sustainable communities for the future.

Among Mayor Smith's grassroots supporters, **Michele McGraw** had made Lynnwood her home in 1988. She thought Lynnwood had a nice family vibe. At the time she was expecting her first child and her home was surrounded by horse pasture. For some time, she had been hearing that Lynnwood would be growing. There was always concern over whether Lynnwood would grow in the right way. Subsequent mayors talked about the growth of Lynnwood, but it was just talk. According to McGraw, "Nothing happened." The shift happened when Mayor Smith was elected. That was a huge turnaround for Lynnwood. "She brought a collaborative skill set with her. She was very collaborative. A strategic thinker. Very genuine. The decisions she made ... things actually started happening. And that was fun to see."

Sound Transit 2, adopted in a 2008 ballot measure, approved several light rail projects, extending the light rail northward to Northgate by 2021 and to Lynnwood by 2024. Sound Transit 2 also casts the light rail east to Bellevue and Overlake. Sound Transit became the foundation underlying the need to develop a city center in downtown Lynnwood.

Once Sound Transit 3 was ratified in 2016, planning expansion to Everett, the race to the future was on. Ensuring that the City of Lynnwood was prepared for the explosion of growth was Mayor Nicola Smith's chief priority. She knew that this surge of unprecedented growth would impact every facet of the city and everyone who lived or worked there. "Growth is inevitable," she said. "And I want to make sure the changes are in the best interest of everyone. We manage the growth. We don't let the growth manage us."

Mayor Dave Earling said, "Greatness is about to be thrust upon Lynnwood whether she likes it or not." It had been very frustrating for Lynnwood that the city didn't have a seat on the boards of either Sound Transit or the local transit provider, Community Transit. For Mayor Smith to get a seat, first she had to get on the board of Community Transit, then Snohomish County Executive Dave Somers could appoint her to the board of Sound Transit. There are 18 board members on Sound Transit.

Mayor Earling, one of the original board members, was on and off the Sound Transit Board for 19 years. Typically, the board members are either mayors, county executives, or city council or county council members. Mayor Smith came into office after Mayor Earling had served his first two years—he took office in 2012. Mayor Earling helped to arrange for Mayor Smith to take his board seat because of the proximity of the light rail to Lynnwood.

"Getting her appointed to the Sound Transit Board really got her thinking about the importance of the region and how Lynnwood fits into the region."

Having the right elected officials on the Sound Transit Board was also important to Sound Transit's officials. Sound Transit CEO Peter Rogoff said, "Whenever we are extending our service into a new city, you need to establish a good working relationship with the mayor and the city council. We have to obtain permits from the city for everything we do. We want to make sure our plans align with the city's plans."

For at least a decade Lynnwood didn't have a seat on the board of either Sound Transit or Community Transit. Ultimately it took the retirement of Mayor Dave Earling to create a spot for Lynnwood. The Snohomish County Executive can appoint three members to the Sound Transit Board. Sound Transit requires that one of the three members must also be on the board of the local transit agency, which is Community Transit. The requirement is to ensure that the local transit system, Community Transit, is synchronized with Sound Transit.

Snohomish County Executive Dave Somers said, "We knew in group discussions several years ago that Lynnwood was the next hub and certainly would be greatly impacted by construction, that is when we first thought about getting Mayor Smith on the board. When Mayor Dave Earling decided to retire that really helped." Mayor Smith was selected to fill Mayor Earling's vacated seat on the Community Transit board and then Executive Somers was able to appoint Mayor Smith to the Sound Transit Board.

"The arrival of light rail by 2024 is going to be transformative for the city," said former **Community Transit CEO Emmett Heath**. Heath had served as CEO of Community Transit until the end of 2020. He credited Mayor Smith for preparing the city, in terms of understanding and planning, for what the light rail station would bring. He also notes that the light rail would transform the city whether the city was prepared appropriately or not. He cites the light rail as one of several factors prompting the city to start their master plan for the city center, the construction of residential housing and additional retail development. "Mayor Smith and her staff did a great job working with Sound Transit and Community Transit on the changes that would come about with the light rail."

Lynnwood was the next hub and would certainly be greatly impacted by construction, there was never any question that getting Mayor Smith on the board was the right thing to do.

"Mayor Smith is sharp and engaged, so she was the perfect choice anyway," Somers said. "We had to be thinking a year out to get her on the Sound Transit Board. I remember even during her days at Edmonds College, she had a lot of support in the community and that transferred over to her role as mayor. Sometimes you get into political actions over the appointment of board members, but in her case, there was great support for her."

Some critics suggest the board members are not elected by the people, but it is important to keep in mind that they are already *elected* officials. There are some positive aspects to being on the board of Sound Transit but some negative aspects too. "It's not a golden crown," Somers suggests. From the perspective of an elected official, it has some pros and cons. Mayor Smith had access to the city staff who could give her the facts about the impacts of Sound Transit and the City of Lynnwood: the demands for housing, impacts on businesses. And yet growth and development can raise the ire of people who do not want to see changes in their community, especially those changes that bring in a new influx of outsiders and impact the status quo of government services. According to Michele McGraw, Mayor Smith was collaborative and involved. "She put people in the right place where they could have a positive impact."

Mayor Smith proactively put Lynnwood on a larger stage by interacting on a regional level. With the inevitability of the light rail coming to the city, she made sure that the city's position and voice was being heard in the region.

Lynnwood's **Human Resources Director Evan D. Chinn said**, "Her amazing ability to collaborate with local and national leaders, including other local mayors and public agencies. She's done a good job of connecting and maintaining relationships with those leaders."

As County Executive, Dave Somers notes that he has the staff and a number of resources that he can bring to the countywide meetings so that they are able to ask questions and develop strategies.

"Mayor Smith is a great team player," he said. "All of the impacts to Lynnwood fell into place. And she's just been great."

Other elected officials in Snohomish County also acknowledge that Mayor Smith is good for Lynnwood, but her collaborative efforts have also spread outward to the county. By sitting on the board for Sound Transit, she has also negotiated a regional agreement. **Representative Cindy Ryu, MBA (D-32nd)** commented, "Nicola is well respected among leaders in south Snohomish County. She has a sterling reputation for being fair and inclusive and for working for the betterment of everyone in the community. When she picks up the phone, everyone answers her call. She listens and is inclusive of other perspectives—that is what makes her a strong regional leader."

Representative Rick Larsen represents Washington state's 2nd Congressional District, which includes portions of Snohomish, Skagit and Whatcom counties and all of Island and San Juan counties. Representative Larsen serves on the House Transportation and Infrastructure Committee and the House Armed Services Committee. These committees enable him to focus on creating jobs and opportunities to meet the local needs of northwest Washington. He views Lynnwood as one of the larger cities in south Snohomish County and thinks it's important that Lynnwood take a leadership issue on the one thing all of the cities have in common— Transportation.

Larsen has observed Mayor Smith continuing to push for the light rail links and at the same time, she has moved forward on the new Community Transit orange bus line. She has also placed her emphasis on bike and pedestrian infrastructure.

"After she got her feet wet as the mayor and had the understanding of what it would take to run the city, she realized that to be an effective leader for Lynnwood she had to be an effective leader for the region," he said. "One thing that has been important is more of an emphasis on the City of Lynnwood in a regional role. When you represent people, you do have a voice beyond the boundaries of your own city as well as for the benefit of the region."

Mayor Smith took her service on the Sound Transit and Community Transit Boards very seriously. She is not a board member who only perks up when the issue pertains to Lynnwood. She is inquisitive and cares about issues in other areas, Bellevue, West Seattle, Everett—the entire region. With or without Mayor Smith, Lynnwood would have gotten the light rail. The difference that came about because of her leadership is that for a long time Lynnwood did not have regional relationships or a regional presence, and now they do. She put Lynnwood on the map. She built trust and relationships with other elected officials and that had implications far greater than planning for the light rail.

Chapter 11
The City of the Future is Here

At just under 8 square miles, 16 square miles including the Municipal Urban Growth Area annexation area, the sprawling bedroom community had always been a car culture. Previously known as a place just to go shopping, Lynnwood was now getting squeezed from all sides and had no choice but to grow up. Washington state's population increased, more than doubling in size, and job growth surged on the Eastside in Bellevue and Redmond. By 2035, the Lynnwood area was projected to have a population of over 92,000 people, including 54,400 people within the current city limits.[3] Lynnwood straddled the nexus of I-5 and I-405, where the huge job centers of Seattle and the Eastside brought tremendous opportunities to the community. With the coming light rail, renewed attention was given to the roads. But that's not all. Mayor Smith and her staff began to look at local transportation options connecting commuters to Lynnwood's neighborhoods.

Safety has been deemed to be the No. 1 issue for the Lynnwood community, whereas in the past the community seemed more interested in the state of the city's roads. To argue that safety and roads are two separate areas of concern does fail to connect the dots. Mayor Smith knew that Public Safety encompasses more than police and fire services. Well-traveled roads that are well maintained are at the crux of Public Safety.

One of Mayor Smith's colleagues, **Mayor Barb Tolbert** of Arlington, has provided leadership through the financial crisis as

---

[3] "Snohomish County Tomorrow 2016 Growth Monitoring Report: Population Growth Trends" (PDF). Snohomish County Tomorrow Steering Committee. March 22, 2017. p. 21.

well as the SR-530 Mudslide, also known as the *Oso Mudslide that* took the lives of 43 people in 2014. Mayor Tolbert has a keen understanding of the complexity and risk management that goes into running a public entity to keep everyone safe and healthy. "The No. 1 risk area to cities is generally roads: managements, accidents. Maintenance—this is the biggest area of exposure," she said.

The Lynnwood Public Works Department is bigger and more complex than Lynnwood citizens might imagine and has an engineering department, construction managers and internal department managers. This Public Works Department oversees the city's roads, streets, parks, water system, sewer system stormwater and wastewater treatment facility. The department also manages street traffic signals. Maintaining the city's municipal buildings and its fleet of vehicles, trucks and cars is also a function of Public Works.

Public Works Director **Bill Franz** has been with the city since 1991. He was originally hired as an entry-level civil engineer. Through the years he rose through the ranks and found his way to the director slot in 2004.

"When I first got to Lynnwood, Mayor Meryl "Herk" Hrdlicka was still mayor," he said. "I saw the respect people had for him. He was very influential. He had been mayor for about 28 years."

More than anyone, Bill Franz is aware of the changes made to the Public Works Department under Mayor Smith. "We've become a full-service Public Works Department. Public Safety—infrastructure of all of the basic systems that provide the daily wants and needs of our citizens." Bill Franz is clear that one message Mayor Smith has carried throughout her years is her wish to break down silos between functions and departments. "Before Mayor Smith, if you said Public Safety, people would assume they meant Police and Fire. She made sure that there are portions of Public Safety that run through every department." Franz also notes that even how the department budgets for outcomes, and how the department spends money, function across departments. "These key functions are not confined to this department or that department," he said. "It is the whole team that is involved to create success."

Mayor Smith and the city council spent a lot of time figuring out how to properly fund road improvement and road maintenance. Former City Council Member **Rev. M. Christopher Boyer said,** "The easier it is to get around the city, the happier people are, just to have decent streets to drive on. The condition of the roads is much better. One example is the 196th Street widening and improvement project."

Early on in her first term, Mayor Smith challenged the leadership team to come up with a seven- or eight-year plan so that when light rail arrived the city's roads were prepared to meet the new commuter demand. Bill Franz said, "Under her urging, we developed an overarching capital plan—a list of projects and a funding plan and carried that into each subsequent budget. We have a ways to go, funding is always something we try to figure out but we've had some success." According to Franz, successes include "36th Avenue West—a huge win $17Million and 196th—east/west route – a huge win. $50 million, brought in $25 million in grants— outside money."

Mayor Smith understood the importance of building infrastructure by strategically planning what needed to be done before the light rail opened. Significant changes have already been made and that has had an impact on private real estate development. Bill Franz thinks his finest work as the **Director of Public Works** has centered around helping the city council and the Lynnwood community to have an understanding of infrastructure and how to fund it. "Think of bridges falling down," he said. "Our department has worked really hard to get the council to understand infrastructure—the things that are deteriorating can't always be seen. It might be roads failing underneath the pavement or utility poles are rotting inside. It's the unseen things that we keep an eye on. There are lots of needs to ensure Public Safety. Our team looks at all of these needs."

The Public Works Department is vigilant about maintaining roads so when people are driving, and they have to make a split decision, things are clearly marked, and drivers immediately know where they should be or shouldn't be. There are things that the Public Works Department is vigilant about—that citizens might not even know about: making sure the Lane markers on the streets are crisp, the street signs are clean and reflective, potholes are filled, tree limbs are trimmed…the list goes on.

Sometimes small details tell a larger story. George Smith, who has retired from Edmonds College, lives within walking distance to Lynndale Park. He frequently walks through the park to get some exercise. Everywhere he turns, there are fir trees and huge maples. "I enjoy my walks in the park. With all of the trees, I breathe deeper. I enjoy seeing the pups running in the dog park. Whenever there are branches blown down after a windstorm, they are quickly swept up. I can rave about the City of Lynnwood. The city does a nice job of upkeep."

One day he noticed there was a big hole in the side of a tree. He could see where the tree had opened up and split. The next day while he was on his walk, he spotted three workers from the city. He told them he thought the tree could be dangerous if it ever came down. Three or four days later, the tree had been cut down. "If you take a look at the center. The middle 10 inches is completely sawdust—the tree was rotten to the core. I call it my stump now," he said.

George Smith has called the city a few times when other things like that have happened. "The city has been very responsive during the times I had to contact them about something," he said. "It's one thing being a good citizen and quite another having the city respond that way."

Roads are in a state of constant flux and require vigilance to maintain and to meet the high requirements of Public Safety. Tatyana Sineeva's work and lifestyle require her to do a lot of driving. Between her commitments to her business, her son's Boy Scout troop and her Russian Orthodox Church, she sees the city from many different perspectives.

"Under Mayor Smith, the city has parks that are in good shape and more bike lanes. Lynnwood playgrounds are in great condition with new turf," she said. She also notices that the city's roads are still far from perfect. "The city is run really well," she said, "Except 164th, there are holes all over. It is dangerous to drive there. The contractor did not do a good job. They need better road thoroughfares around Alderwood, but that was inherited from the prior administration. It is a small bottleneck there. Roads are not designed to handle the new development and traffic flow." Sineeva also noted the improvements that are being made. "But 36th Avenue has been improved and works well. From Alderwood to 161st Street, they made this road beautiful."

Building infrastructure around transportation requirements encompasses more than road construction and maintenance. **Road improvement plans often take 10 or more years to design and implement.** 196th St and 44th Avenue would continue to serve as major thoroughfares for the city center. The 196th St SW Improvement Project has begun construction. This project will enhance this important arterial from 48th Avenue West to I-5 with City Center standards, by adding two additional business access and transit lanes, medians for safety, wider sidewalks, and landscape features with a boulevard appearance. This project aims to help ease congestion, accommodate growth in the city center and create a better, safer place where people could walk.

As a part of the City Center development, additional improvements are being made to current side streets, and new streets will be developed in order to improve traffic flow, walkability and bikeability. For instance, 42nd Avenue West is a planned new street that will connect **196th St SW to Alderwood Mall Boulevard** The city received a $3 million infrastructure grant from the Puget Sound Regional Council for this project to be used for the design phase.

The Poplar Way Extension Bridge was another project that would help alleviate congestion and keep traffic flowing in and around the city center. **This new arterial bridge over I-5 will connect Poplar Way/196th St SW to 33rd Avenue West.** The city received over $3.2 million in federal and state grants for the design and an additional $3 million in federal grants for the right-of-way phase. This project remains a top priority for the city and the region as additional federal funding is sought.

Upgrades and improvements to the city's water and sewer systems were also made to the city center and mall areas. These improvements allowed for a significant increase in sewer capacity to accommodate the new growth anticipated over the next several decades and keep everything flowing the way it's supposed to.

Without a doubt, construction is an inconvenience, but progress can't be made without it. Mayor Smith often asked the community for their patience as these improvements were made.

Gunnvor Tveidt, who owns the small business Talent Services, said, "People are upset about streets being torn up, but under Mayor Smith, work has started on improving the city's roads and streets."

The mayor also worked side by side with Community Transit as they planned to start building their network into the communities where people live and work so they can get connected to Rapid Transit. She also envisioned adding bike lanes and walking lanes. "In the long run, we will save people time and money and create a healthier environment," she said.

Community Transit provides more public transit in the City of Lynnwood than in any other city in Snohomish County. Community Transit's Emmett Heath said, "Our staff and their staff have always had a relationship, but it was extremely productive under Mayor Smith." The working relationship between Community Transit and the city focused on street-level changes, building new facilities, and making sure the traffic flow in and out of the light rail station was efficient and seamless. Heath said, "Mayor Smith hired a great staff, and she was a great role model for the collaboration for so many partners to work together to make it happen, building sidewalks, transportation networks, bike networks and street networks."

The light rail station in Lynnwood was designated to be the Northern Terminal Station, a hub. The modeling done by Sound Transit projected that it would be one of the busiest stations with 18,000 to 20,000 boardings per day. The transportation network needed to be coordinated for pedestrians who walk there, or people who bike there, drive their car and expect to park there or arrive by bus. Mayor Smith and her staff were planning for the arrival of the busiest station in the entire Sound Transit network. Peak ridership was expected in the morning and in the afternoon when people were going to work and then going home. A lot of midday ridership was anticipated as well. Emmett Heath stated, "The statistic we used to quote in order to serve the passengers coming and going—one of our CT buses will be arriving or departing the station every 30 seconds."

When it came to making Lynnwood a more livable and community-friendly city, no detail was too small to consider. Planning encompassed more than improving roads and connecting Community Transit buses to the light rail station. Pedestrians needed wider sidewalks and walking trails. There also had to be abundant opportunities for bike access. **Kathy Coffey,** executive director of Leadership Snohomish County and an integral member of Partner Lynnwood, asserts that Mayor Smith was committed to creating a higher quality of life for Lynnwood. One way she committed to this higher quality of life was by creating bike paths. The intention was to make the city more connected. "She brought in experts from Sweden and Denmark to talk to them about how their city was bike-friendly; all of this was all stemming from her desire to connect people," Coffey said.

The new transportation infrastructure became the sum total of the pedestrian, bike, car and shared-ride systems. Lynnwood would no longer be only a car culture. The vital new network that encompassed public transit would become fundamentally important to Lynnwood and also serve as a lifeline to other suburban and urban communities. The long-awaited major development for the Lynnwood City Center began to occur under Mayor Smith's leadership. Going forward, the construction of residential housing and the addition of retail mixed-use space began to take shape. Development of the city center began in 2015, with the construction of two apartment buildings and a hotel located near the convention center. Both she and her staff did a great job working with Sound Transit and Community to make sure the traffic flow in and out of the light rail station was efficient and seamless. "Our vision for the city center is a vibrant central core with mixed-use residential and commercial space that is easily accessible by pedestrians, bikes and cars," Mayor Smith said.

Until 2021, **Grant Dull** had been the executive director of the Public Facilities District (PFD). Most people do not know that the city does not own the Lynnwood Convention Center and the surrounding retail area. The PFD is its own entity, separate from the City of Lynnwood. The Lynnwood Convention Center had opened in 2003 at the intersection of 196th Street SW and I-5. Historically speaking, Lynnwood had always wanted to build a convention center but was unable to get financing. Grant Dull said, "It's hard to get residents of a city to tax themselves to benefit people who do not live here. Out-of-towners spend money on hotels and restaurants, but the revenue (spent by tourists on hotels and restaurants) doesn't benefit the residents enough for them to want to tax themselves."

When Lynnwood learned of the Public Facilities District (PFD) provision, they formed the first PFD. The PFD did issue bonds backed by the revenue stream from sales taxes and lodging taxes. The PFD has never had to rely on the city to make its debt payments. Lynnwood was able to build a convention center that was a win-win. It generates stature for Lynnwood as a growing asset without relying on the city to pay any of its debt. As an added benefit, no new taxes were levied on the citizens of Lynnwood to build the convention center. "So, the whole rationale for the convention center worked out well," Dull said.

Grant Dull recalls how the relationship between the Convention Center and the city has changed since Mayor Smith has been in office. A few years ago, one of the Convention Center's largest events, for The Northwest Aerospace Alliance, had been slated for March. Then Snowmageddon hit. "I was desperately trying to get a private snowplow service to plow our parking lot," Dull said. He sought help from the city, knowing it was way out of bounds. He recalls having a conversation with Mayor Smith. She decided that it was in the best interest of the city to have the parking lot plowed. "That was a conversation that I could not have had under the previous mayor," Dull said.

The impact that the light rail and the development of the city center will have on the Lynnwood Convention Center remains to be seen. The light rail will stop at the downtown city center, but the next station will be at Alderwood. Grant Dull observed that "The development of Alderwood with its new housing and expansion has become a nexus of activity."

There will not be a light rail stop at the convention center. "We haven't solved that issue yet and I don't think most people are aware of that issue," he said. He envisioned Lynnwood returning to its roots and creating a trolley system that would go from the convention center to the college to the light rail terminus. "Most cities have something in their legacy that they can hang their hat on. Edmonds has their waterfront. Lynnwood doesn't have a sparkling legacy, but it can resurrect the Lynnwood Trolley."

Mayor Smith's working relationship began with her long career at Edmonds College. During her two terms as mayor, the city fostered a deep community bond with the college. It is only fitting that her relationship with the college is examined within the context of the changing infrastructure in the Lynnwood community. Kathy Coffey, who was involved with Partner Lynnwood, recalled that Mayor Smith wanted to make sure that road access to the college was easy.

The President of Edmonds College, **Amit Singh,** has been an astute observer of the growth in Lynnwood. He serves on several committees to stay in touch with the development of the city center, housing, especially the building of the homes and apartment complexes, near the mall and at the mall. Amit Singh has also observed how Community Transit is working on a new express line, the orange line that will connect the city of Mill Creek with the college campus. A new terminal is being built on the campus that will go to the light rail. "Mayor Smith's leadership has been great for this area," he said. "Her focus is on what is good for the city, what is good for people and what is good for everyone, people of color—what will help lift everyone. It's not about politics or one group or the other but what is good for the city and to face the challenges and to solve them. That is something that is refreshing about the City of Lynnwood."

Immediate infrastructure changes to Lynnwood included Sound Transit's Lynnwood City Center Station Parking Garage and Community Transit's new Orange Line Bus Rapid Transit. But the changes that came as a result of private investment and private real estate development quickly mushroomed. City center development included the development of landmark housing and retail projects: The City Center Apartments, Destinations Senior Apartments, the Hilton Garden Inn, and the project called Kinect @ Lynnwood. Two new projects at Lynnwood Square included The Northline Village and Lynnwood Place. The vicinity surrounding Alderwood saw two new projects: Avalon Alderwood and the Alderwood Mixed-Use Project. Two brand-new additions to the Edmonds College Neighborhood are Triton Court, built to house students, and Hazel Miller Hall designated for STEM education.

One explanation for the ease and efficiency of the changing face of Lynnwood can be attributed to the newly reorganized DBS that combined four of the city's functions into a single department with streamlined customer service. Simplifying and making the business application and permit process accessible online has made a difference. Restructuring to create DBS is something Mayor Smith worked on from the beginning of her tenure.

Even with the development of 1,000 affordable housing units in Lynnwood City Center, there is still a great need for more. Washington State Senator Jesse Salomon (32nd legislative district) has been working on initiatives to create incentives to develop more affordable housing around light rail. He was thinking about the teachers, waitresses, and the laborers that have to drive two hours to and from work every day and wanted to provide them with the ability to take mass transit to live where they work by developing more affordable housing around light rail. "It's not a high demand area for development but will be a high development area for use so we're trying to bridge that gap," he said.

He has been crafting a bill, a multi-family tax exemption for affordable housing incentives (MFTE). Specific policies include allowing zoning density around light rail stations, and forgiving property taxes for a number of years for developers if they keep buildings at a market rate of affordability for a number of years. He has been shooting for a 99-year property tax exemption for the development of the building. "I haven't been deeply involved with

Mayor Smith on a policy level but more on a political level, generally agreeing that we support mass transit, light rail and the density around those stations, also, social justice and equity in housing and the benefits that can provide."

Representative **John Lovick** has always attended Mayor Smith's annual State of the City address. He couldn't help but note that she always invited other local elected officials. She also always attended his State of the County events when he was Snohomish County Executive. "She made sure we were able to get the light rail spine to Lynnwood," he said. "Look at the growth, the housing and the city center. All of the growth is carefully managed."

The desire for a city center has been going on for decades, long before Mayor Smith came to office. A lot of infrastructure had to be done and that takes time, but Mayor Smith was determined to get the work done. "Our future generations, my grandchildren and your grandchildren will have a way to quickly get around the region to take care of work and school in their day-to-day lives," she said. Some projects have taken flight because of the relationships Mayor Smith built with different people and agencies—that have opened doors. She built this foundation so Lynnwood could move forward. Tatyana Sineeva said, "the city is still moving forward with the right balance of businesses and road improvements. People now say you live in Lynnwood—that's a good place!"

Chapter 12
All Are Welcome

If you want to know more about your city, then get to know your mayor. It is the mayor who sets the tone for a city's culture. Mayor Smith's support of the "All Are Welcome" mandate was more than a seminal message, but part of her vision that grew over eight years and manifested itself in practical goals for the city. Every Wednesday afternoon she reserved that span of time to meet with anyone who wanted to talk to the mayor. Her open-door policy invited new ideas as well as problems that needed to be solved. She kept her ear to the ground and learned what was needed by the community.

Art Ceniza, who sometimes describes himself as her "co-pilot," said, "She is not the typical political person. She is unique as a public official." Every Wednesday she met with anyone who made an appointment. "She was willing to meet with everyone and anyone, even her political enemies," Ceniza said. "She met with people who had completely different political ideas and kept her door open."

The open-door policy was one of the chief reasons why Leah Jensen wanted to become the mayor's executive assistant. Leah Jensen kept the mayor's calendar and scheduled the meetings. If you brought a problem to the mayor, she was known as the person who could find a solution. The ability to go right to the mayor worked really well and it was very effective. Visitors came from all walks of life: Boy Scouts, Girl Scouts, people coming in to offer their service as volunteers and people with problems. Before Mayor Smith, City Hall wasn't an open and welcoming place. Now the new message to the community was: "We serve you. Not vice versa."

"The ones I have enjoyed the most—when leaders from immigrants would come in and introduce themselves and their community to Mayor Smith. We met with a group from Ethiopia and formed a friendship city with a city in Ethiopia. The mayor met with the Fiji Community and was invited to a huge celebration that she attended with her husband and chief of police Tom Davis." Jensen describes screening the mayor's calls and learning of frustrated residents who felt as though they had gone through normal channels but didn't get anywhere. When Jensen scheduled the meeting with the mayor, whatever city department was involved—those staff members were also invited to the meeting. The intention was always to find some sort of solution. "We never had anyone walk away dissatisfied," Jensen said.

Mayor Smith's open-door policy has made a lasting impression on city council Member **Christine Frizzell**. Frizzell is also a mayoral candidate for 2021. Frizzell recalled one time when she had signed up to meet with Mayor Smith. Another man was waiting in the lobby. I asked him what he was there for. *The city did some road work and now my sidewalk doesn't match the other side of my property*, he told Christine Frizzell. When the mayor's assistant took Frizzell back to her office, she could see through a window into the mayor's office and was surprised to see the man talking not only to the mayor but a director and a deputy director were also in the meeting. "Every city should have a mayor like her—bringing people together to work on a solution together—that's such a vivid recollection for me," Frizzell said.

The mayor's open-door policy was indeed symbolic of authentic changes that were taking place in the city's culture. The influx of newcomers brought a new dynamic to the city—they were younger, energetic and wanted to be engaged with the community. Mayor Smith led several initiatives to harness the power of Lynnwood's diverse community and to build an inclusive environment, where people want to live, work and play.

From 2012 to 2017 Lynnwood has seen a large influx of immigrants and young families. Lynnwood is getting young families who can't afford Seattle anymore and now want to raise their children in Lynnwood, where there are good neighborhoods, good schools and plenty of space. The addition of the light rail will further increase growth. By the time the next census comes, the population of Lynnwood will have increased tremendously. Edmonds School District Board Member **Dr. Deborah Kilgore** has observed how the city is diversifying. "If you look at the demographics, it has changed significantly," she said. It is so important to govern as things are— the realities of having a diverse constituency means we have to change the way we do things, so everyone is served equitably. To envision it. Mayor Smith has done a good job of getting everyone on board with it."

Mayor Smith saw that there was a great demand to create a new Diversity Equity Inclusion Commission (DEI) so that its work could meet the needs of the Twenty-first Century. Seven commissioners were unanimously confirmed by the city council. The new commissioners were a group of young people with young families who wanted to be involved for the right reasons. They understood institutional racism and barriers to access. They also had a network of people they could connect with in the Lynnwood community. "DEI Commissioner Naz Lashgari remembers starting her work in June 2017 and going on with different Programs that the commission had envisioned. "We have been very busy in the last four years under Mayor Smith's leadership in collaboration with HR Director Evan Chinn, moving racial and social equity forward," Lashgari said. "Mayor Smith was ahead of her time making sure there was a DEI commission to make a difference in the city and its culture, to make sure everyone knew about it."

Led by the **Diversity, Equity & Inclusion Commission (DEI),** the city launched the "All Are Welcome" initiative. This initiative turned into a guiding principle as the city worked toward becoming a more equitable city. As both a branding and messaging statement, the *All Are Welcome* design is a colorful and tangible representation of the city's commitment to being a safe, welcoming and equitable city for all people. Mayor Smith said: "We have this beautiful imagery and language, letting our diverse community members know that they are welcome, valued and appreciated and that they belong here."

The ***All Are Welcome*** wrap was created by a collaboration between the DEI Commission and the Arts Commission. The new signal box wrap was added to the city's public art collection. The *All Are Welcome* wrap was placed on the corner of 184th Street South West and Alderwood Mall Parkway. Signal box wraps were added throughout the city—outward signs demonstrating what it means to be an inclusive community.

In addition to making the community feel safe and welcome, the city took deliberate steps to make its internal culture a safe and welcoming place to work. There was an initiative made for city employees to reflect the diversity of the community. Steps were taken for the HR department to be more intentional with recruitment and retention. An internal committee was created called LEED - Lynnwood Employees Embracing Diversity. LEED's mission was to cultivate and promote a welcoming, safe, equitable and inclusive workplace for all city employees.

The city also provided its employees with training and opportunities for dialogue to normalize talking about race and inequities and finding solutions to create justice. **Human Resources Director Evan D. Chinn** said, "She has redoubled her commitment to the city to be a safe, welcoming and equitable place. She has steered the city in that direction. That was part of her campaign promise. Laying out this mission and vision of the city has been one of her accomplishments, especially relevant during all of the happenings around racial inequality and social unrest around the country."

To further the goals of creating an equitable city, Lynnwood joined GARE – the Government Alliance on Race and Equity. GARE is a national organization that works with governments to help advance racial equity at the local government level, and Lynnwood was the first city in Snohomish County to become a GARE member. The Lynnwood GARE cohort comprises 12 employees from all the departments of the city and includes all levels of the organization from maintenance staff through department directors.

Naz Lashgari commented, "In the last four years that I have been with the city, I have seen a more diverse pool of employees joining the city employees. We are still 68% white but we see more diverse people joining the city. Just the fact that diversity and equity and inclusion are being talked about—all of this makes a difference"

The team has adopted the name Team REAL (Racial Equity Advancing Lynnwood) and learned effective approaches to eliminate institutional and structural racism and advance racial equity. The work of Team REAL continues as the city began to apply its antiracist learnings to the city's policies, procedures and projects. Mayor Smith said, "I am all in. Lynnwood is all in, and that includes our council leadership and chief of police and department directors. I stand with our communities of color and all those who have been marginalized, and I commit to doing better. We've come a long way but recognize that there is still a long way to go."

Under Mayor Smith's Leadership, "Lynnwood became three WWWs," **Rep. John Lovick** said. "Warm. Wonderful. Welcoming." Lovick explains why he feels that the city became more welcoming. Shortly after Mayor Smith took office, there was an event held at the fire station honoring Black History Month with a reception for the Black community. Mayor Smith had invited John Lovick to speak at the event. "You can't see stress. You can't touch stress. But you can always feel stress and I could feel stress in the room," Lovick said. He recalls seeing the former police chief at the event. Back then the Lynnwood Police Department was not known for its diversity. Mayor Smith spoke about making Lynnwood warm and accepting for everyone. "Lynnwood had never felt warm and welcoming for me until she became mayor. Lynnwood is now a warm and welcoming city for people of different ethnic, racial and LGBTQ minorities."

After the murder of George Floyd, Mayor Smith participated and supported a peaceful protest led by Joshua Binda. Public Works cleared city streets so the protestors could lie down on the street for nine minutes and 29 seconds. The mayor's views on social justice have had a lasting influence on her family. Her daughter Emily participated in the march, along with her granddaughter Kendall and grandson Julian. The mayor was touched and proud to see her next two generations of family carry forward the same values. Mayor Smith has mentored and endorsed Joshua Binda in his campaign to become a Lynnwood City Council member. If elected, he will be the youngest (21 years old) Black council member in Lynnwood city history.

Mayor Smith and her staff also focused on the Americans with Disabilities Act (ADA). The city was also working to make the community safe, welcoming and livable by meeting and surpassing ADA standards. The city worked on a plan for bringing all city facilities, sidewalks, curb ramps and parks, including the city's communications, policies and programs, to current standards and to be accessible and welcoming for all users.

Creating a culture of inclusion meant finding a special place for veterans in the Lynnwood community. The needs of veterans are not always addressed by municipalities, organizations or institutions of higher learning. The reasons for that are manifold and might be attributed to the changing nature of the military from conscription-based to all-volunteer troops.

Regardless of the reasons why the needs of veterans are often ignored, Mayor Smith recognized that veterans needed to receive special recognition for their service to the country.

Her work with veterans stemmed back to her days at Edmonds College. At that time one of her colleagues was **Peter Schmidt**, who was initially an associate dean, and he also happened to be a veteran of the Air Force. Together they worked to support services being offered to veterans at the college. After she became mayor, she asked Peter Schmidt to come to the city to lead a roundtable. The purpose of the roundtable was to learn how the city could better serve veterans and their families. "That was history in the making for the City of Lynnwood," Schmidt said. "We invited people from Lynnwood and south Snohomish County executives, and representatives from the Department of Veterans Affairs. We hosted a full agenda, and we took a look at what it means to be a veterans-supportive city."

According to Peter Schmidt, it takes more thought and deliberation to say we are supportive. "After that discussion, we launched into the vision, mission and values, and the next steps. We asked what we needed to do to move ahead. Who will keep the initiative going? Who will champion the effort? Nicola took that work and kept it going. A white paper was created as a foundation and then it was built upon. The next step was the founding of the Veterans Museum—she gave it life."

Of all people, **Zabine Van Ness** thinks she should be the last person in the world to launch and conceptualize a Veterans Museum. She was born in 1942 in Nordenham, Germany and had never lived in a *free* Germany. During her entire time that was spent in Germany, she could not understand why people had voted for Hitler. She said, "I thought: *Why?*" A devout believer in the Bahá'í Faith, she has spent an entire lifetime asking that question. She called Mayor Smith because she wanted to help her by volunteering with the Diversity Commission. Van Ness is the founder of The Unity Museum that is located in Seattle's University District. The museum offers rotating exhibits and special presentations on both local and global topics that represent the advancement of civilization.

When the mayor learned that Zabine Van Ness had started the Unity Museum, she asked her to start a Veterans Museum. Van Ness said, "I asked her for a couple of names. I sought a place that was affordable in Heritage Park and volunteers. Then within three or four months, the whole thing was together, and it opened. I insisted everything was free, free coffee and cookies. Then the veterans started to come."

When **Gina Israel** worked for the City of Lynnwood, she had one of those long titles: Intergovernmental Liaison at City, Sister Cities and Veterans. She had been hired by the city to do a pilot project. She was responsible for doing outreach to legislatures and coming up with a sister city program. She was also doing a lot of relationship-building with different communities, including the veterans' outreach. Gina Israel recalls Mayor Smith giving her approval to move forward with both the Northwest Veterans Heritage Museum and the Heroes' Café—to build a veterans' hub in

Lynnwood. "The intention was to give veterans a brick and mortar—a one-stop-shop for veterans' services." There was also the creation of the South Snohomish Veterans Taskforce, comprising seven or eight volunteers to help administer social services to veterans.

Until recently, **Chris Szarek** had been the veterans coordinator at Edmonds College. Today he is the college's newly appointed executive director of facilities and capital projects. At the time of this writing, he was still in the process of handing over the Veterans Center. He recalls the enormous pride he felt when Mayor Smith first invited him to be part of the city's roundtable on veterans.

"She called a group of veterans into her office to meet because she wanted to make Lynnwood a great place for veterans to live. All of us were honored to be there. We brought a lot of people I knew together, and I met people there for the first time that were veterans or worked with veterans. We wrote a lot of ideas that day. This is great, but it's a lot to do. How much of this would get done? But when you look at all the things that we said we wanted to do, it's heartening to see how many of those ideas have been put into place."

The veterans started a Heroes' Café, where they hosted guest speakers and programs. Mainly the café became a special place for veterans to meet and build camaraderie. Catholic Community Services also became involved. The café became more than a gathering place but provided one-stop services for medical care and education. Since its inception, the Heroes' Café has moved around to a few different locations. At one time they met at Verdant Health Services. When they met at Verdant, there were services available for veterans seeking employment, veterans' benefits or housing.

Chris Szarek said, "Some veterans don't want to be part of any organization, but they could come to Heroes' Café. We have people at Heroes' Café that served in World War II, Korea, Vietnam, and all branches of the service. We have breakfast, coffee and lunch. We tell stories and share time with friends." Right now, the Heroes' Café is located at the New Life Church. They've already outgrown their current space and are raising money to build a larger place.

Lynnwood was selected as the site for a new Gold Star Families Memorial, which will be installed in Veterans Park. The process of getting selected was described as competitive; Lynnwood was chosen because of the city's track record of supporting its local veterans. Early in her term, Mayor Smith had committed to being a Veteran-Supportive city, one in which the city's local heroes could live, work, play, get educated and, most important of all, thrive.

The Gold Star Families Monument is a tribute to the families of the brave servicemen and women who have sacrificed their lives in the name of freedom. "Our most important job is to make sure we're not forgotten," Chris Szarek said. "We need to put things in place, so it is in place for the next generations, so it doesn't go away when we are no longer there. We're leaving behind an infrastructure and a legacy."

Inclusiveness takes many different forms. One way a city can be more welcoming of its diversity is by establishing formal relationships with its ethnic communities. These relationships can travel far beyond the city's limits and evolve into Sister City and Friendship City Programs. **Yun Hong** has known Mayor Smith the entire time she has been an elected official. He said that he really got to know her when she ran for reelection.

Once the CEO of a shipping company in Seattle, today Yun Hong is a motel business owner and the chairperson of the Korea Association. Through the association, he does whatever he can to help Korean Americans who live in Snohomish County. He was very impressed that Mayor Smith had reached out to the Korean-owned businesses in Lynnwood. He cited her as being one of the few caring people who appreciated their community.

"She had the background from being dean of international students," Hong said. "She was very sensitive to minorities. We were very impressed. We asked her to get involved in our community in a celebration of any kind. She was eager to participate. As mayor, she made us welcome in the community. I found her to be very compassionate to a minority group and she genuinely cared for our cultural backgrounds."

When Mayor Smith established a Sister City program with Damyang, South Korea, student exchange programs were coordinated through Edmonds College. Yun Hong and his wife Kay

Shin traveled with Mayor Smith and her husband Del to spend five days together in Korea. Yun Hong remembers being very impressed by how Mayor Smith represented not only Lynnwood but America. During the trip, Hong's wife Kay Shinn acted as translator. "When you travel you really get to know people," Hong said. "The people of our companion city, Damyang, were very impressed with our soft-spoken mayor and, yet, she was quite open and charismatic, a caring person. In Korea, they did not expect a lady mayor to represent the City of Lynnwood. All of the political people were very impressed, and I was very proud."

Soon two new Friendship City Programs were created. City Council Member Julieta Altamirano-Crosby facilitated the formation of a Friendship City relationship with **Chilpancingo, Mexico and** most recently in 2020, Lynnwood joined in a new Friendship City relationship with **Bole Kefle Ketema, Wereda 10, Addis Ababa, Ethiopia**, with support from the Lynnwood-based Habesha Community Center.

Creating these relationships is a great way to appreciate, value, and celebrate the various cultures in the Lynnwood community.

County Executive Dave Somers said, "She really understood how in Lynnwood there are many income levels and diverse communities. She's worked to recognize that and make sure everyone's included, everything from businesses to her thinking about the people in her growing community. She respects the people, so no one gets lost—that's very front and center for what diversity means."

At the end of the day, people don't necessarily like change. They want equity, but not if it significantly changes their lives. Change can bring a lot of resistance. A number of people who have worked closely with the mayor have described her innate nature as always being one of a change agent. Linda Jones, president/CEO Lynnwood Chamber of Commerce, said, "Lynnwood has changed in many positive ways, and that is good to see!"

As a focused leader, Mayor Smith kept pushing forward and made those hard decisions. Part of her legacy has been transitioning Lynnwood from being solely a white-centric culture to becoming a community that is much more inclusive and diverse. She has done a good job of getting everyone on board with it, even people who might not like change. A welcoming community begins with a mayor who not only opens her door but who also **opens her heart.**

Chapter 13
Women in Leadership

Even before she became mayor, Nicola Smith loved her community. She was not afraid to do the things that she asked other people to do. She was known for her compassion, but her sense of caring was grounded by her common sense. She thought about how her decisions would impact people, lots of people. She was not afraid of being wrong. She has a low ego, not a lack of ego, but her need to govern was not borne of a craving for power but firmly rooted in her desire to serve, to take care of things, to be a steward who left her city in a better state than she first found it.

"She leads with her heart," Shannon Sessions said. "That can be a negative but, in this case, it is a positive."

Women are making strides toward greater political participation on a global scale. However, in many countries, women are vastly underrepresented in politics, specifically in local government.[4] The first woman mayor in the United States, and in the world, is Susanna Madora Salter, who served as Mayor of Argonia, Kansas, in 1887. Salter ran for mayor soon after women were given the right to vote in municipal elections. She was known for her commitment to the Women's Christian Temperance Union. Several men jokingly nominated her to run for mayor on the Prohibition Party ticket. To everyone's surprise, she won. As it turned out she knew a great more about politics than she had let anyone know and performed exceedingly well as mayor.

---

[4] The International Republican Institute is an American nonprofit, nonpartisan organization committed to advancing freedom and democracy worldwide by helping political parties to become more issue-based In the United States. https://www.iri.org/
https://www.democracyspeaks.org/blog/women-mayors-make-difference

Fast forward into the 21st century, as of May 2021, population data from the U.S. Census showed of the 1,621 mayors of U.S. cities with populations over 30,000, 407 or 25.1%, were women. During 2014, the year when Mayor Smith first took office, there was a surge of women mayors elected into office from Oregon to Canada.

As women are obtaining more leadership roles in municipal government, it's essential to examine if they lead their cities differently from their male counterparts.

"Women need to be asked," said **Rep. Cindy Ryu.** "Men become politicians because that is what they envision. They don't have to be asked, whereas women have to be asked. Sometimes they have to be asked many times. Women run for office, not to seek power, but they see a need to step up because they know they can make a difference."

When Nicola Smith was being asked to run for mayor, there were those like Jean Hales and Theresa Poalucci, and others among her Rotary circle, who thought she stood a great chance of winning because she was a woman—that women have an advantage over men at the local government level. There was no doubt that since Nicola Smith had excelled as an administrator in an institution for years that she could take those same skills and experience and easily make the transition to city government.

Those who support women assuming leadership roles seem to know that women have the right skills to do a good job at governance. **Mayor Barb Tolbert** (Arlington, Wash.) said, "Women tend to be problem solvers, that's much more of a natural skill set. We're solving problems every day, particularly when we have families. We focus on solving problems to make our families run smoothly. And those skills transfer so well to the community."

Almost every city up and down western Washington seemed to have a woman mayor. "We were a majority female leadership group which was unusual and impactful," Mayor Smith said. "Women mayors changed the culture of government leadership, almost overnight and in some instances, it made men anxious."

Shannon Sessions recounted how Mayor Smith's leadership style put her in a vulnerable spot. There were times when the mayor did not talk and instead listened. The experience she had gained over the years told her *when not to talk.* According to Sessions, "Her naysayers would say. 'She's not leading or letting the directors do everything. She has her hands in things that she doesn't need to be involved in.'"

In Sessions' estimation that was the best narrative her critics could devise. "When someone is so good, this is the narrative that they came up with—it was the best they could do, even if it's not true; if you say it enough, then people might say it's true." Sessions thought there were naysayers who would take the city back eight or 12 years before Mayor Smith came to office.

Past mayors of Lynnwood had leadership styles that often drew scrutiny for being more combative than collaborative. When Mayor Smith ran for reelection in 2017, she was interviewed in a League of Women Voters' radio show with her political opponent George Hurst. He claimed that she deferred to her department heads because she must not want to be a strong mayor. Hurst criticized her for the same qualities that others had attributed to her successful leadership.

Mayor Barb Tolbert said, "Everything about being a man or a woman in politics has changed. Communities have lost their ability to operate civilly. What happened to that process, the community was able to give up their accountability for their words and actions? There was a time when the community would have stood up against negative discourse, but the community has abandoned that responsibility. Society has complex problems. Change gives everyone a reason to be on edge."

Representative Cindy Ryu thinks Mayor Smith is bringing civility back into city government. "She commanded it as a leader in the City of Lynnwood. Prior mayors had used their positions as platforms for what they personally wanted done."

On the topic of women in leadership, Senator Marko Liias commented, "Prior to Nicola, a lot of decision-makers were older white men. She brings a collaborative leadership style. This is a space where she has worked hard for both her community and for the region to find a path forward that serves everyone well."

Aside from serving as a member of the Washington House of Representatives from the 32nd District, Cindy Ryu is also the current chair of the Women in Government Foundation. Serving women legislators for 31 years, the foundation provides a forum so women in government can learn from one another. "Once women are in the seat of power, they get things done," Ryu said. "If they are no longer needed, they get out of the way. Women have more common sense and use their seats in a way that is practical."

Prior to Mayor Smith taking office, Lynnwood's representation and presence at the state level with the state legislators was nonexistent. Once she came to her post, the city began participating and made certain that they were getting representation. As mayor, she also made sure that her staff was involved and represented the city, so that Lynnwood would be top-of-mind among legislators and other electeds, especially when it came to seeking federal and state grant funds for infrastructure projects. It was Mayor Smith's collaborative leadership style, exercised internally among her staff and externally among her colleagues in government that built her reputation as a servant-leader.

Senator Marko Liias said, "There is something unique about the inclusive leadership style that women have learned and exhibit instead of the territorial style led by some male leaders, particularly because mayors have a great deal of authority in their city. Often, they need to control things outside of their boundaries by building those bridges and building those connections that impact both their cities and the surrounding region."

Enough research has not yet been done on the collaborative leadership style that is exhibited by both men and women, but especially with women. The mayor's role seems to benefit from a collaborative leadership style because so much more can be accomplished by having a strong network of relationships than by working alone in a silo. There is a convergence of women who govern from a collaborative space, and this is, in and of itself, a great strength. "Nicola fits in that mold," Senator Marko Liias said. "To use an expression from boxing, she punches above her weight."

A mayor is either collaborative or not. The mayor is the one who shows up at every event, offering the desire to serve and collaborate.

Mayor Jon Nehring (Marysville, Wash.) said, "No one forces me to do this job, but if you're going to do it effectively, then you give up a lot of personal time. You can't do it half-heartedly—that's what it takes to be collaborative and to be a regional leader." The mayor spends many weekends and late nights, volunteering, participating in community events, going to community fundraisers, and establishing relationships with nonprofit and other community groups. If collaboration is a priority, then a mayor does these things consistently. "I hope collaborative is one descriptor people would use to describe me," Mayor Nehring said. "Whether it's public and private sector or cross-county collaboration we are stronger by working together. If we flounder around, trying to do it ourselves, we will not bring real or lasting solutions without that collaboration."

The mayor of Lynnwood is a nonpartisan position. A mayoral candidate might be a member of one party or another but does not run as a representative of that political party. There is always pressure to be a Republican or a Democrat, but the mayor can't hide behind the party and play politics. Consequently, mayoral leadership is done through a nonpartisan lens. And it's a nonpartisan role for a reason. The mayor has to make decisions for the best interest of the entire community and that can be challenging. The mayor has to have compassion for the community she serves and recognize where she can make a difference.

According to Mayor Cassie Franklin (Everett Wash.), "Mayor Smith focuses on where she needs to make a difference—Public Safety, economic development, equity inclusion. She works within all of these goals and doesn't get distracted from her ability to make decisions."

Cassie Franklin took office January 1, 2018, becoming the first woman to be elected Mayor of Everett. Mayor Franklin is a local and regional leader. She serves on the Puget Sound Regional Council, the Economic Alliance of the Snohomish County Board of Trustees, and the Executive Board of the Greater Seattle Partners. In 2018, she was appointed by Governor Jay Inslee to the Choose Washington New Mid-Market Airplane Council and was one of just 36 individuals selected to participate in the Department of Defense's prestigious Joint Civilian Orientation Conference. Prior to becoming mayor, Franklin was elected to the Everett City Council in 2015 and served as the council's Vice President in 2017.

Mayor Franklin has observed that "Women are far more collaborative, and they enter into the political world with a lot less ego. When we lead, we focus on what we need to do to solve the problem, instead of who will get credit for the solution." Mayor Franklin has also noted that at times the less collaborative mayors are the ones who become isolated. She asserts that the public needs mayors to work together. "Being a good mayor requires a person to have a collaborative nature."

Mayor Franklin has worked with Mayor Smith in the South Snohomish County Mayors. The group takes a collective focus on the region and the opportunity to exchange ideas and advice to support their leadership in their own cities. "I'm glad to have Mayor Smith as my fellow mayor and my sounding board," Mayor Franklin said. Mayor Barb Tolbert observed that since the time when so many women mayors were elected, the dynamics of the group have changed. "Collaboration became easier," she said. And Mayor Matsumoto-Wright (Mountlake Terrace, Wash.) described why she and Mayor Smith clicked right from the beginning, "We felt that we had the same values."

Mayor Franklin recounted how she had been on a morning call with Mayor Smith and other mayors in the county. Mayor Smith shared her dilemma with the group. She had heard from members of her Ethiopian community in Lynnwood, who were traumatized by what's going on in their country of origin in Tigray, in northern Ethiopia. Prime Minister Abiy Ahmed of Ethiopia had invited forces, including the Eritrean army, and they were massacring the people of Tigray. Mayor Franklin said, "She invited us to listen— that is what a woman does. Maybe it is the way we are wired. Women lead with a lot more compassion."

The leadership traits that make a good mayor don't always produce instant results. Good leaders have to be patient and willing to work toward goals they might never see to fruition. They lay the groundwork for development projects that might take 10 or 15 years. Mayor Franklin stated, "In Mayor Smith's case, the results of some of the things she has laid the groundwork for, will be seen in 10 or 15 years—the downtown city center, equity and inclusion and making Lynnwood a welcoming city."

It is incredibly challenging to be a woman in leadership. Mayor Jennifer Gregerson (Mukilteo, Wash.) said, "I've heard from a mayor who predated my service who commented that the South Snohomish group felt like a boys' club." Mayor Gregerson also meets with the other mayors who are part of the South Snohomish County Mayors group. Regarding women in leadership positions, she said, "For me, the cities where the leadership has changed to having a new woman mayor, there is a willingness to openly communicate, a willingness to collaborate and the desire to improve relationships in general."

The leadership traits that make a good mayor encompass softer skills such as listening well and learning, having empathy and being decisive. According to Mayor Gregerson, being collaborative only goes so far, then the mayor has to resolve a situation, and be willing to stand up for it. "With a mayor, you're everyone's boss. You have to trust the people who are around you."

Christine Frizzell points out that with women leaders, "There is more emphasis on relational leadership instead of top-down leadership." Other women whom she admires in leadership positions include Michelle Obama, Ruth Bader Ginsburg and Mother Teresa. "All of those women are strong. There is a strength about each of them," she said. "And there is a strength about Nicola—she doesn't shy away from what is hard and faces things."

Mayor Smith has always had a group of people around her to whom she could float ideas. Amazing things have happened during her tenure. She is the one who facilitates these things to happen. "She gives these ideas life and gives people permission to move forward with good ideas. That is really a special aspect of Nicola,"

Shannon Sessions said. "Because of her, we have been opening doors that we would not have otherwise happened without her. She honors the gifts that people have. She lifts them up for that."

A strong leader inspires people to do things they might not have believed they could do. Women who are in leadership positions are setting an example for the next generation of women. Young women are out there, watching and listening, patiently waiting for their turn to come. They see what is possible to accomplish for themselves and for their own communities. "I hope to inspire young women who are taking leadership roles," Mayor Smith said.

Reimi Pieters began working for Mayor Smith as an intern. Within a few weeks, there was an unexpected opening for her to become Mayor Smith's executive assistant. Reimi Pieters was delighted to have a full-time paying job for the summer, but she was also concerned because she had not had that much work experience and this was an important job. "She didn't coddle me or treat me as in any way lesser because I was only 20," Pieters said. "She expected me to fill the role as it had been assigned to me. She knew that I could grow in the role. The idea of being held at a higher standard encouraged me to take the position as far as I could."

During the time that Reimi Pieters worked for Mayor Smith, she observed that the mayor was compassionate, listening to the concerns of her staff and other department heads. "At the same time, she was very firm when it came to her expectations of what she wanted her staff to do, or the results she wanted from her staff," Pieters said. "She did trust her staff to take individual ownership and as a result, a lot of creative ideas came forth. She let her department heads be experts in their own department as long as they met her expectations for the best interest of the city."

Mayor Smith's leadership style is "rooted in communication," said Sarah Olson. "Mayor Smith was always prepared and spent a lot of time making sure that communications are well done. She just doesn't just go into a meeting. She is able to communicate real ways we can collaborate and offer solutions because she prepares herself for the moment." Changing the city's culture took hard work. Mayor Smith was clear about articulating what she wanted for the city's administrative culture and expected her directors to be on board. She also believed in developing people and giving them opportunities to be successful.

Kyle Funakoshi said Mayor Smith has always been willing to mentor. "She garners and engenders trust. That is one of the important things that mentors do." He describes how she had always recognized his strengths but was also willing to call him out on those things he needed to be called out on. "I was glad when she was elected mayor because I didn't have to worry about my neighboring community, what their values were and what kind of people were leading the city. We need more leaders like her. I'm hoping the people she has mentored in the past will step up and become that next generation."

Mayor Smith commended Reimi Pieters' performance at the end of the young woman's summer term. She told Pieters that she had the potential to lead and to make a difference in her chosen field. "Just having that belief in what I could accomplish in my career helped me to reach bigger goals—that made a big difference in my career path for me, as well as it did for others too." For female leaders to acknowledge when they see potential in someone is very empowering. Strong role models are not only authority figures but look out for others and help them to see their own potential. The practice of setting expectations is really valuable. Being able to meet those expectations is empowering. The impression that Mayor Smith made on Reimi Pieters has stayed with her. "I took that to heart then and still do."

Chapter 14
Call me *Nicola*

Mayors are human beings who have homes, spouses, children and pets—personal lives, sometimes wonderful, sometimes exasperating or messy, just like all the rest of us. The friends, colleagues, and family of Mayor Smith have consistently described her as having dual abilities that were extraordinary—to stay focused and to listen well. Everyone in her inner and outer circle has concurred, above all other factors that she has always exuded the warmth and caring that is missing in most politicians. Her executive assistant, Leah Jensen, said, "She has a soft side I haven't seen in a lot of female leaders. Women in leadership roles don't show that softer side of themselves. Nicola has a lot more grace."

Then there is the *Nicola factor*. She didn't really want to be called Mayor Smith. Being *Nicola* was at the core of her identity.

"In meetings with Lynnwood Employees Embracing Diversity (LEED) issues, she found herself thinking and telling them: 'When you call me mayor, I lose a piece of my identity. I've got the mayor hat on and I can't take off until I'm no longer mayor. Call me Nicola.' They understood I had lost some of my culture and identity."

Who is Nicola Smith, the woman?

She will tell you she is the oldest of four siblings, "the bossy one." Her birthday is March 15, the Ides of March. For history buffs, the Ides of March was considered by the Romans to be the deadline for settling debts. The Ides of March is best known as the date when Julius Caesar walked into the Roman Senate alone and was assassinated in 44 BC. Roman tragedy notwithstanding, the personal life of Nicola Smith has not been without adversity.

Of English and Scandinavian descent, a native of the Pacific Northwest, she has a sister and two brothers. Her mother emigrated from England to the United States via Canada. "There is a whole cultural story there," she said. Learning of her own mother's emigration story has always inspired her to have compassion for immigrants and refugees. The rest of the family is living in England. She and her husband Del married in 1984 and are coming upon their 37th wedding anniversary.

Many people have described Del Smith as her rock. They were married at her parents' home that looked out on the water, across to Vashon Island. He remembers doing a lot of gardening in preparation for their outdoor wedding. "We had friends who had a sailboat and scurried us away on our honeymoon. We traveled down to the Oregon coast for a week."

From the onset, Del knew his wife was a strong woman. They both worked at Edmonds College in two completely different departments, where they seldom crossed paths. Del said, "Her background at the college, managing large budgets, personnel groups and departments, transitioned easily to city government because that's exactly what the city needed when she was asked to run for mayor."

Del has enjoyed his wife being the mayor because it brought him the opportunity to go to places and meet people he ordinarily would not have met. "He's enjoyed the ride with me," she said. After working in IT at the college for 20 years, Del has retired and spends a good deal of time doing photography. "For the most part, we've had an easy life together," she said. "We have two daughters and four grandchildren."

Nicola's closest friends describe her as the one who brought people together and was always the one to get the job done. **Gay Hardy** has known Nicola for 50 years. They went to middle school together. She remembers that her parents lived in a house on Maplewild road in Burien that went back in the family for a hundred years. Gay calls her *Nicky*, the girl who had beautiful straight blond hair that was always perfect. They both went to Highline High School in Burien. After high school, Nicky went to Denmark for a year and later went to college. They both went to the University of Washington around the same time. They went to Europe together and traveled for six weeks. "Nicky has great hands. She can make anything. She has a fine sense of order. She can organize anything. She can take a pile of crap and make it look like a million bucks. It's a real talent. And she likes doing it."

Of the four children in the family, **Ruthann Esterly**, the youngest, works in her own furniture refinishing business with her husband and lives in Seattle. "I'm the little sister that was a pain. I was the baby of the family. Nicky was amazing. She was also a pain in the butt. She kept me in line." The older brother, **Paul Berglund**, has been a Bering Sea fisherman, a chief steward with 120 people on board, and started fishing as a purse seiner when he was about 12— as a cabin boy. "I traveled around the world," he said. "I've been in the jungles of Cambodia." He once stayed with the Awá tribe in the Amazon rainforest in Brazil. "I've been in Indonesia and worked three jobs to get where I wanted to go." Once he went to Hawaii and got a job on a marlin boat. "I've had a lot of adventures out to sea," he said.

Paul Berglund says that he and Nicola always had a bond. "I was much different, but we always got along." He spoke of how his sister was always academic and driven to succeed. "At the UW she worked very hard for good grades. Even though she was always striving and worked hard, he never thought she'd be a politician. I didn't see her going into politics. They came to her to ask her to run for mayor. She did not do it 100% of her own volition," he said. "Nicky does well with organizational stuff and is not afraid to pull the trigger. She's got empathy which is a good thing. She's done a good job with where Lynnwood was and where it's going to be."

Ruthann Esterly recalls one of her favorite memories of her older sister. Nicola had been living in Denmark on a student exchange program. Her family, including Ruthann, went to visit her in Denmark. Ruthann said Nicky was playing a song on the guitar, *Leaving on a Jet Plane*, by John Denver, made popular by Peter, Paul and Mary. "It was funny. Nicky was always leaving on a plane to go somewhere," she laughs.

Ruthann describes the birth order of the siblings: Nicky is the oldest, then Paul. "I'm the youngest." She doesn't mention her other brother, Michael. Paul does talk about his younger brother. "Michael committed suicide, but he was a fantastic dude."

Michael died in 2012, the year before Nicola ran for mayor. She called him 'Serious Mike.' He did well. He and his wife once had a nice life together. He got his degree and had his own construction business, but he couldn't cope. He self-medicated and sank into drugs and alcohol. Paul remembers Nicky helping him cope through his illness by offering him work and support, yet Michael worked at trying to take his life for a couple of years. One day he hung himself in his ex-wife's garage.

George Smith, who worked with Nicola at Edmonds College, remembers that she was devastated by the loss of her brother. Nicola's childhood friend Gay Hardy said, "Her personal life has had its fair share of real tragedy and hardship, yet she was able to accomplish amazing things." Losing her brother was the first of several other tragedies yet to come. How well Nicola Smith managed the city, while enduring one personal crisis after another, speaks volumes about her strength and integrity.

Her youngest daughter Tia had a drug problem by the time she was in the 7th Grade. Her addiction was traumatic for both Nicola and Del. They had a similar experience with their older daughter Emily who had also had a bout with drug use when she had been in high school in Granite Falls but had recovered. Emily moved away from Granite Falls to separate herself from her group of friends who were into drugs. Emily's grandparents invited her to live with them in Burien while she finished high school. Nicola's mother drove Emily from Burien to Granite Falls every Monday and supported her with home schooling the rest of the week.

Colleen Pruss lives in Granite Falls in Snohomish County and is a retired medical social worker who used to work in a nursing facility. She's close to Nicola and Del who used to live across the Pilchuck River, northwest of her in Granite Falls. Colleen Pruss' own daughters Lydia and Madysen were friends with Emily and Tia. The girls were young then. Colleen's friendship with Nicola began when Tia and Madysen became pals in kindergarten. Later, Colleen ran a day care years ago and took care of Tia for four years. "When I had Tia in my child care, I left a note on my door, 'We're down by the river.' We had picnics there."

Colleen Pruss remembered the days when their respective families vacationed on the beaches of Oregon. Pruss said Nicola introduced her to the importance of family vacations. Nicola didn't just make food. "She offered all of these different foods. Cultural immersion experiences. Shabu-Shabu. Indian Food. Good old-fashioned American barbecues…" People came from all parts. Sometimes Nicola's cousins came. Her niece came from England. Nicola's parents visited for the day. Del's parents came for the day. "The family was always about including friends and good caring people. Colleen's dad and stepmom came and her mother-in-law from Iowa and her sister-in-law, the list of people who came was endless. Pruss had memories of beachcombing, building sandcastles, eating ice cream at Tillamook, renting horses and riding on the beach, exploring tide pools full of sea life, anemones, starfish, and seeing the glow of the sunset light up their daughters' faces at night.

"We have strong family connections. We love our families. Nicola's friendship has been a huge joy in my life—it's a once-in-a-lifetime friendship. We've been emotional and have cried at times, but we have laughed way more than we cried."

When Colleen Pruss talks about Tia's addiction, she gets emotional. "Tia is one of *my kids,* so it's an emotional topic for me. It was difficult to watch the emotional toll that Tia's addiction took on Nicola and Del. Nicola did counseling to work through those really personal issues, but she never gave up on Tia. She tried and tried. She kept on trying different things. It was difficult for Nicola and Del and it was a long time. It took years."

"Tia's addiction was a dark hour for all of us," Del said. "She was in trouble early on when Nicola first became mayor." It would be hard on any parent, but in this case, Tia happened to be a daughter of the mayor.

TJ Brooks is a retired police officer. "I saved her daughter Tia," he said. Brooks had spent 30 years with the Lynnwood Police Department. He describes being the law enforcement liaison for the drug court "as the most exhilarating experience." People who were arrested for narcotics had a choice of going to drug court or being tried for a felony. Successful completion of the program meant they had graduated to become *clean*, drug-free. Every week Brooks evaluated each person's status. If they violated the terms by using drugs, then there were consequences. "It was a great program," Brooks said. "I learned so much about being compassionate about people who suffer from addiction or mental health issues."

Frantz Jocelyn Donat always seemed to mysteriously appear at pivotal moments in Nicola's life, almost as if he was her guardian angel. Frantz Jocelyn Donat remembered seeing his mayor alone in her office one day. She had been crying and he wanted to know why.

"A mother, her daughter," Frantz Donat said. On a deep intuitive level, he understood the pain his mayor was experiencing. "Then I remembered somehow at that moment, God walks his way, our way." He saw the pain in her eyes and told her Tia would be coming home. "She's going to be OK."

Frantz Donat believes that to be a leader you have to have a lot of wisdom and the mayor has wisdom. "She listens," he said. "We all have to learn to listen to have wisdom. Mayor Smith has that wisdom."

Tia did return home to her mom. Tia eventually enrolled in drug court and got clean. About her mother, Tia said, "I think that once I realized that she was on my side and always has been—that made me open up to her and she was able to support me."

Tia and her partner have a baby—Elijah was born in April 2019. The couple soon found an apartment around the corner from Nicola and Del's house. Elijah, who is now a toddler, has become a symbol of Tia's recovery.

"I'm proud of all of them," Colleen Pruss said. "Tia is so in love with her son. It's a huge relief for Nicola. She often says, this baby saved your life."

TJ Brooks had opened the door for Tia to enroll in drug court and it successfully changed her life. "There were setbacks," Del said, "but Nicola and I never gave up on our daughter."

Nicola saw clearly that addiction impacted people in the community from so many different walks of life. She saw the carnage that drug addiction had caused not only with her daughter but with the community. Once people get into the legal system, it's hard to get out. If people end up in jail, they get turned out onto the street with no support. They are often released from jail during a time when a family member can't come to get them and help them get away from the drug environment. They have no recourse but to get back in touch with someone who is involved with drugs. "As the mayor and as a mother, people and police said to me, 'I know what you're going through.'"

Tia found that her own experience with addiction had given her mother the chance to explore what could be done. Tia said, "By witnessing firsthand what had happened to me, motivated her to make a change for people who were suffering as addicts. It motivated her to help more. It inspired her to do the work that she does."

Nicola made a profound and lasting commitment. Donning her mayor hat, she said, "The addiction problem crosses all boundaries, lifestyles, groups and economics. I've been able to work through the system and help people. I don't see why we can't fix it."

A new item appeared on the Mayor's Fix it List and she asked her daughter to help her. Tia knew the current group of children who were cycling through drug court. Her mother asked, "Do you think your group would come and talk to me about their journey and anything we could have done differently to offer support?" A new roundtable was formed. Six young adults came to share their stories; so did EMTs, the police and other community leaders. "I was very proud of my Tia for organizing the event and I was proud of the others for coming. Maybe people make mistakes but with help and compassion, they can get back on their feet. By working with the police, we see how we can be more supportive."

Toward the end of Mayor Smith's second term, Tirhas Tesfatsion took her own life while she was incarcerated on the site of the older Lynnwood Jail facility. It was the first in-custody death at the Lynnwood Jail since its opening in 1994. Tirhas Tesfatsion's tragic death further bolstered the need for the new Lynnwood Community Justice Center that was already beginning construction after two years of development and design. Mayor Smith responded by appointing a task force with the support of LPD Chief Jim Nelson, Representatives Lauren Davis and Cindy Ryu and Senator Jesse Salomon to reimagine the planned 114 jail beds of the new Community Justice Center by dedicating a section of the new facility to be designated as behavioral health beds.

Snohomish County set a record for overdose deaths to date in 2021. The county lost 232 sons, daughters, moms, dads, spouses, and friends to drug overdoses that could have been prevented. The Lynnwood City Council met over a six-week period to deliberate over the implementation of behavioral treatment beds in the new justice center. Tia Smith was invited by Representative Davis to give her input as part of a community focus group.

Tia has seen her mother experience all the phases of life, her accomplishments, the caring and the joy. She also witnessed her mother's struggles, setbacks and disappointments, the human side of being a woman. Her mother persevered, weathering the storm, always forging ahead.

"She's strong. She knows how to put her game face on and keep on going. That doesn't mean she pushes things aside. She talks to us and lets us know her emotions. But when it's time to do the work, she doesn't let anything get in the way of that. She's strong-willed. She's organized. She's good at planning. She's always planning things weeks ahead. She has done a lot of great work. She is a great woman, great wife, great mother, and a great role model for me. She taught me everything. I'm strong because she taught me how to be strong."

During her first term as mayor, with the exception of having had eye duct surgery in 2016, Nicola's health was good. Then, one day things changed. It was July 11, 2018, Wednesday, the same day of the week when she held her open-door meetings. She heard those words a woman dreads hearing after she's discovered a lump in her breast. She was diagnosed with having a malignant neoplasm, estrogen receptor-positive. Cancer.

"I was in denial," she said. "I didn't have time for cancer as mayor. Why on earth did I get cancer. My dad had prostate cancer;

my mother died from leukemia. No one in my family had breast cancer. I decided that it was because of stress."

She remembers the most pressing issue happening was with the fire district consolidation. She worried that the consolidation would go sideways because of some of the personalities. Her fire chief, Scott Cockrum, was getting tired or burned out from trying to make the project make sense to people. Without the consolidation, the city would face a huge budget deficit along with the other cities in the region. So many fine details still needed to be worked though. She had already worked countless hours on the consolidation. It would have been a real disappointment if it had not come through in the end.

"My staff and the council wrapped around me offering emotional and healing support," she said. She scheduled the surgery during the city council's recess. Surgery was performed to remove the lump August 22, 2018. Beginning in October she had 30 days of radiation treatment. Five days a week, she drove to Everett for treatments.

While she was undergoing treatment, it was business as usual. She and her staff were preparing for their Standard and Poor Rating Conference. She was chairing the Snohomish County Cities Group. In September the city held the South County Fire inaugural ceremony establishing the Regional Fire Authority. Work had begun on the Rodeo Inn Project to be a site for homeless children. The city, led by the mayor, welcomed a group of high school students from sister city Damyang, South Korea. She was also in the midst of undergoing efficiency studies with several city departments.

All of the staff in her inner circle were amazed to see how she never wavered from her job. She, in turn, gives credit to her staff: Leah Jensen, Art Ceniza, Julie Moore and others. Leah Jensen said, "Even though she was going through treatment, she still wanted to make her meetings and seldom asked anyone to step in and take responsibility. It was amazing to watch and also very concerning to me. She's not just my boss, she's my friend. I don't know how she did it."

Nicola names her husband Del as her best supporter. "He took great care of me. He monitored all the pills I had to take and cleaned my drain tubes." She remembers that there was a surge of breast cancer cases. Several of her friends were experiencing this same nightmare. One of those friends happened to be Mayor Kyoko Matsumoto-Wright (Mountlake Terrace, Wash.).

The two mayors first got to know each other as colleagues and were both active in the Snohomish County Cities Group. On the personal front, Kyoko's son, Yoshi Wright, had experienced the same problem with drug addiction as Nicola's daughter. Now they shared one more thing in common. Both were cancer survivors. "She's a cancer survivor and so am I," said Kyoko. "Nicola checked in on me. She had ended treatment a year before. My treatment ended in May 2019 and by the end of October, I was done with radiation. She called on me to see if I was OK."

Nicola's cancer was caught early. The doctors jumped on it. She was lucky. "She's on tamoxifen for five years," Del said. "Her recent visit was positive. So, everything looks good. It was hard for me and our daughters to go through."

Around the same time, Nicola was undergoing cancer treatment, her daughter Emily's house caught fire. Emily lives in Lake Stevens with her husband, Greg and their three children. The fire broke out from a pellet stove that had been improperly installed by the home's previous owner.

"We lost a lot of stuff," Emily said. "There was a lot of smoke damage. We moved out and cleaned it out and the remodel took a year. I was pregnant." There was a silver lining. Everything turned out fine. The family was safe, and no one was hurt.

Emily has seen her mother experience adversity on many fronts, including on the public stage. Every step of the way, Emily was by her mother's side during the reelection campaign, often bringing along her children while she participated in campaign activities. She said it was challenging for her mother to be in the public eye, and especially figuring out how to be civil but respectful when smear tactics were being used against her.

When her mother ran for reelection against city council member and business owner George Hurst, she was favored to win. Mr. Hurst had received support and encouragement from Don Gough, the previous Mayor of Lynnwood who lost in the surprise landslide resulting in Nicola Smith's upset victory. Despite Don Gough's loss, he had continued to be a vocal and litigious opponent of the current mayoral administration. His criticism of Mayor Nicola Smith had been widely reported in the Everett Herald and other local press. He made allegations of fiscal mismanagement against her that could not be substantiated.

Michele McGraw remembers receiving a mailer making accusations and innuendos that things were not going well, and money was missing. "It didn't jive with my gut feeling," she said. "And I was like wait a second. What is going on? What is happening in my community? I've been seeing things going in a positive direction and someone is throwing rocks at that!" This realization motivated McGraw to get involved in Nicola's reelection campaign. Prior to that time, McGraw had not been involved in city politics.

Tia also remembers her mother being publicly attacked. When her mother was running for reelection, someone made up a fake news flyer, printed them, and put them on people's doorsteps all over Lynnwood. "People didn't take it seriously," Tia said, "but it hurt her to be falsely accused."

David Kleitsch, who has worked closely with Nicola for many years, noted that because she is genuine and welcoming, she had a challenge seeing that some people are not.

"Some people are devious," Kleitsch said. "That's not who she is, and she has a hard time understanding it. It's hard for her to understand terrible behavior. She tries to work through it or around it—but it is a challenge for her." Kleitsch marveled at the fact that she endured professional challenges while at the same time she faced challenges in her family, and yet she was able to carry both aspects of her life to success. He thought it demonstrated her ability to keep both her life and work in balance and to accomplish two major and important things simultaneously. "It comes from who she is in her core—what is at her core—who she is."

The true test of one's character is how a person responds when confronting personal tragedy. 2020 proved to be a watershed year for Nicola. Her father was dying; he went into hospice at his home. He had bone cancer, some dementia and couldn't walk or even stand. "Not many people knew I was struggling," she said. When you're a leader and have that level of stress at home, it can take its toll. "She had to take care of him," Del said. "She did all of the in-home hospice care before he passed away, and still ran the city as well."

Mayor Cassie Franklin (Everett) had also lost a parent several years ago. "I know how hard it is to be in a position of grieving while you're leading. It takes a lot of strength." She cites the challenge inherent in being a woman in leadership. "We are not allowed to show our emotions or else we will be perceived as weak. If we're strong, we're told we are power-hungry. We are held to a higher standard."

Most people who were in Nicola's orbit during the past few years, knew that she had faced health issues, but they did not know the details. It's hard to bear the weight of challenges that are personal, the messy details of having a family and a life, and still be a strong leader. Nicola didn't necessarily want to share the things going on in her personal life, but it was her nature to be open and transparent. Her work of running the city was never affected. She was always dependable and reliable. The more we can find the balance between being human and being a strong leader, the easier it will be for the next woman who comes along. It's a powerful story to be told for women, for girls, her daughters Emily and Tia, and for her as a mom.

Del is Nicola's primary confidante. "Sometimes I learn more than I want to know," he said. "There is a debriefing after every council meeting. The amount of information is overwhelming sometimes. I tell her when something doesn't make sense. She is able to air things out. She can put it out there and that helps her process—that might work as a solution. Then, she can reach out to her staff and department head and talk about it."

Then came the fall. It was St. Patrick's Day, around the time when she was taking care of her father. She cleaned up her garden because yard waste was being collected the next day. As she hauled the heavy yard waste dumpster from the backyard, she tripped on the lid and split open her forehead. "My husband and Tia were in the house but could not hear me crying out for help. Thankfully, I was able to get up and walk into the house." When Tia saw her mother bleeding from a massive head wound, she took over the emergency. She sat her mother down, told Del to call 911 and got compression on her forehead to stop the bleeding. The paramedics arrived, took her to the hospital, where she needed 15 stitches.

After the fall, it was time for Nicola to take stock of her own life. Del had retired. As her confidante, life partner, her rock, he knew her better than anyone else. If Del had to give her advice about whether she would become mayor all over again, he would say: "Be aware of how much time and work you're going to have to invest in it. It's a 24/7 job. Spending eight hours behind a desk is one thing but keeping the city running is a big job. You're still fussing, doing email, going to council meetings in the evening, ribbon-cutting ceremonies on the weekend, and there is always some event someone wants you to speak at. It's a huge job and it's never done."

There were good times ahead. They had a 30-foot-long trailer that had all of the amenities: a bed, a bath with a shower, a kitchen, TV, microwave, a stove, air conditioning, water heater and a furnace. It's a little home on wheels. "A nice getaway," said Del. "We haven't gone anywhere that we can't get to in four hours. Once Nicola is out of office, we'll go out on the road, a month or two months at a time and head east to a lot of places we haven't seen: national parks, Midwestern and Northern states, maybe even New England. Both of our parents traveled the entire country after retirement. Now we can do that too."

But first, she still had to navigate the city through the worst crisis in its history—the pandemic.

Chapter 15
We are One Lynnwood

At the beginning of 2020, not much was known about the mysterious respiratory infection that had killed at least nine people and sickened thousands more in Asia. Then January 21, 2020, the first known case in the United States was recorded. The patient was a man in his thirties who had spent several months in Wuhan, China. On Jan. 15, the Wuhan traveler took connecting flights from China to Seattle-Tacoma (SeaTac) International Airport to return to his home in Snohomish County. The next day, he began experiencing symptoms of pneumonia; he went to a health clinic for treatment and was quickly transported to Providence Regional Medical Center in Everett.

From the time the Wuhan traveler arrived at SeaTac until the time he was hospitalized, he had interacted with 68 people, but none had ever tested positive for the virus.

While scientists were able to trace the virus to the man living in Snohomish County, they were astonished to learn that the same branch of the virus had already begun to show up in at least a dozen states. On Feb. 3, the U.S. administration declared a public health emergency to respond to the coronavirus outbreak. By mid-February, two large outbreaks of the coronavirus were reported at two nursing homes in Kirkland, Washington.

The virus cut a swath through Washington state. In Lynnwood, over 20 square dancers gathered for a pie and ice cream social to cap off a three-day weekend full of square-dancing events. The Wuhan traveler had not been at the event, nor had any of the event participants recently traveled outside of the country. At least 15 of the dancers became sick with symptoms of Covid. One square dancer, Peter Andersen, was diagnosed with Covid. Andersen, who was in his forties, died March 2, becoming the first coronavirus-related fatality from Snohomish County.

The Covid-19 Pandemic hit Lynnwood hard. The same month Mayor Smith suffered from a mishap and fell, the City of Lynnwood had reported 4,387 Cases (4,068 recovered, 69 deaths.) The mayor stayed in close communication with her community. She thought Covid did make governance difficult, but the problems were not insurmountable. There was an opportunity to rethink how the city did business. Some people could work from home, especially those who had to rely on day care. City workers could telecommute in a way that met the needs of the job. Many things could be done via Zoom. Work gets done.

"Thank goodness we were starting to Zoom our work because I could work from home and cover up my head wound. The pandemic was my biggest concern. Managing my work through Covid has been one of the biggest challenges I've ever faced."

Everything changed with Covid, but Lynnwood was prepared, and not because the city had been preparing for an unanticipated disaster of epic proportions. The city was prepared because so many systemic, organizational and cultural changes had already been made. From the first day the mayor had taken office, she had intentionally created an organization that functioned seamlessly and efficiently. The city could handle a crisis, even a global pandemic.

In any crisis, the mayor has to be able to communicate clearly. Having the right ideas, the right message and the right tone is the *trifecta,* but to implement a winning communications strategy, it was also critical for the city to have the right technology network.

The city's new network had three legs, so to speak, to stand on. The first leg was composed of IT, such as networking, hardware and software. The second leg was a dynamic website that allowed multiple users from different city departments to post important information. The third leg was all of the different ways the city had to communicate news to its community: Lynnwood eNews, printed newsletters and social media (primarily Facebook and Twitter).

The idea for updating the city's inadequate communications infrastructure emerged during the regular open-door meetings held by the mayor every Wednesday. Mayor Smith had only been in office for six months when a young systems engineer, Will Cena, came by one day to see her. "I told her of my concern with the dilapidated infrastructure and the fact that people had a passion to fix things, but their supervisors wouldn't let them," he said. "Mayor Smith did an efficiency study and hired a temporary director—that started the ball rolling to make the change." When the new division manager, Jim Kelly, came on board, he found out about Will Cena's technology and leadership experience derived from his military background. He thought Will Cena should be doing more and promoted him to become a systems manager. The new manager aligned with the mayor to champion the creation of an IT Department—right around the time that Finance Director Sonja Springer came on board in 2015. Today the IT department has a staff of 13 and Will Cena as its director.

Major upgrades made to the IT infrastructure included revamping the city's intranet, new laptops for the city's directors and managers, the acquisition of Zoom licensing, and the development of a new website.

"It was just the right thing to do," Cena said. "Going into the pandemic was so seamless. Prior to then, there were connectivity issues." Cena describes the old website as a homegrown product that was cumbersome for staff to post new information because it required specialized training and knowledge, or the need to have a web developer on staff. "Our staff acted as project managers and handled the technology," Cena said. "Julie Moore handled the content side. And we fixed the issues."

Will Cena described the real heavy lift as being the creation of the content for the website. Julie Moore said, "The goal was to create as many resources as we could." The development and design of the new website started in mid-2019.

Having the resources available on the website allows people to do things on their own time, not only from Monday to Friday, 9 to 5, when we're available," Moore said. Those words proved to be prophetic. The website was launched in February 2020, the month before the pandemic took off full throttle. Soon people were no longer able to do things in person and needed to have online access to information.

"It's so much easier to find things, to share information and to make updates," Moore said. The website won the 2020 Government Experience Award from the Center for Digital Government for its outstanding website redevelopment and online services. Mayor Smith noted, "The launch of the new website was fortuitous because it allowed our community members to stay up to date with Covid news and information, including health and safety guidelines."

The IT department worked with all of the city's departments to ensure that all of the city's departments had access to technology. For example, the police department had more people who still had to work out in the field, but the command staff who worked behind the scenes had access to laptops and could telecommute. The court system was transformed by technology. Users could sign up for their court session, log in to a Zoom session, and talk to their public defender, a private attorney or the prosecutor. The court was able to communicate with the jails. An online calendar system allowed the public to create their own meeting times and have the ability to log in for online sessions. "I can't say enough about my staff. They were very instrumental in making this happen," Cena said.

The city's Emergency Operations Center (EOC) had always been managed by the Lynnwood Fire Department. Once the Regional Fire Authority (RFA) was created, the team did additional training sessions. South Snohomish County Regional Fire and Rescue continued to be a key strategic partner to the City of Lynnwood as Lynnwood's community fire department. Lynnwood Police Dept.'s Deputy Chief Chuck Steichen was appointed to oversee the command structure of the EOC as its emergency management director. Once Covid hit, the Covid Response Team was prepared. Julie Moore talks to someone on the command staff every day. "We were ready," she said. "We were prepared. We were responsible." According to Moore, other cities were impressed with Lynnwood's Covid Response Team. "I hear from other cities that Lynnwood is exemplary."

Shannon Sessions suggested that because Covid had initially hit so close to home, the city was able to jump into action much quicker and at a deeper level. She also acknowledges that it wasn't only Lynnwood's proximity to the epicenter of the virus, but the fact that the city had already built the relationships with South Snohomish County Regional Fire and Rescue and the Snohomish County Health District.

"It felt like we were already prepared." The city had a liaison on the Snohomish County Health District Board—facilitating the city's Covid response. "When something big and bad happens it's not the time to build the response—we were already there." Sessions commented that the mayor listened to her experts. "The mayor has always been a steady force through this and moved forward."

Aside from being a member of the Snohomish County Council, Stephanie Wright also serves as the Chair of the Snohomish County Health District Board. The board had its first outreach March 2—the same day the county had its first coronavirus-related death. Many issues were raised. "How do we shut down? What do we shut down? Schools? Employers? We had to make sure we were in touch with major employers, like Boeing." Wright noted that it was the last time that the Snohomish Association of Cities and Towns group would meet in person. "Nobody had a pandemic playbook; we had each other as resources, and we tapped into existing resources and relationships." Wright remembers Nicola as being more independent. "Lynnwood had a strong emergency management background. I have to credit Lynnwood with a lot of my emergency management knowledge. It's why the fire services are now under the RFA. Nicola was a strong and sturdy leader."

To ease tension and allay fear, the mayor spoke to the people frequently, asking for their help to get through the pandemic to build a better, stronger community. Many new protocols and policies quickly came into play: wearing a mask, social distancing, limiting gatherings and avoiding large crowds. Vaccines were given to front-line health care workers. The Emergency Operations Center (EOC) Team closely tracked the virus. The city distributed over 35,000 masks. The city's website had a webpage dedicated to updating changing public health guidelines and health resources. Seventy of the city's employees were working remotely. The city distributed $1 million in social relief funds to small businesses and worked with utility customers, offering assistance with utility bills.

Mayor Smith commented, "The entire staff has stepped up to keep the community safe. Police work crews. Internal teams. Information technology and human resources team."

The final toll that the pandemic has taken on the city still remains to be seen. The true impact on small business is incalculable. The city's budget had been challenged, primarily due to the decrease in sales tax revenue. The projected budget shortfall was $1.5 Million. Mayor Smith called for a reduction of spending in all departments. Even greater transparency was given to the city's finances. Keeping the city financially sustainable throughout the pandemic was probably the biggest challenge. Costs needed to be reduced wherever possible. Early separation plans were offered for some employees to create vacancy seatings. These positions were not filled to keep the city financially sustainable with reduced revenue. Some personnel had to be laid off. Cost savings ideas were implemented in all of the departments. Careful planning and prudent management allowed the city to weather the storm.

Mayor Smith said, "Being a mayor in Covid, I have never worked this hard in my life. Running the city and keeping our services open and accessible to the public was a matter of life and death."

Mayor Dave Earling commented that one of Lynnwood's "big gifts was Alderwood Mall." It is estimated 41 or 42% of the city's revenue was derived from sales tax. And while there was a projected 11% decrease in sales tax revenue in 2020 during the pandemic, it turns out that the sales tax dip was not as low as originally forecast. Even during the pandemic, shoppers continued to flock at Alderwood, albeit masked and maintaining social distance.

Despite all of the health and safety protocols, forced closures, stay-at-home mandates, and the pervasive fear of catching Covid, people had to live their lives. All along and prior to the pandemic, the Lynnwood Parks Program provided ways to connect with the community. Now the Parks and Recreation Department was charged with the task of keeping the community safe while offering new opportunities for recreation.

The city had not forgotten about elders and shut-ins who had been dramatically impacted by the pandemic. New programs engaged seniors and the housebound with weekly phone calls and friendly check-ins just to stay in touch. Remote learning programs also served seniors and a community that had grown increasingly isolated and lonely during the pandemic.

The new city website made it possible for staff to easily post news about new programs and all the other ways the department continued to engage with the community.

The Director of the Parks and Recreation Department, Lynn Sordel, said, "We kept our parks open. We kept our parks safe. We ran our summer camp. We had all kinds of protocols and safety requirements. All of the things that we did for the community were amazing." Sordel notes that the mayor trusted him and his team and saw the value in their work—that the things they were doing during the pandemic were really important. "And we got great feedback from the community," he said.

For the past several years, and long before the pandemic hit, the city had been working hard to improve the quality of its parks. Lynn Sordel spoke of the work that had been done to examine the parks according to a breakdown of economics and demographics in every neighborhood. The results led to a series of maps that were incorporated into a long-term plan to improve and reimagine the parks.

"Creating the maps was the spark for the city to create a plan to make the parks more welcoming."

The plan led to the renovation of South Lynnwood Park, which was in the city's most racially diverse neighborhood and in need of a major overhaul. The city reached out to the local community to gather ideas about what people envisioned for their park. The renovation expanded the playground, added new picnic shelters and seating, resurfaced the tennis court, made ADA improvements to the restrooms and pathways, added an artificial turf soccer field and a new bike station, improved drainage of the grass and natural areas, and included new public art.

Making Lynnwood more beautiful had been one more item on the Mayor's Fix it List. She saw the value in creating beautiful parks and green spaces, not solely to be aesthetically pleasing, but as one more way to instill a sense of community. A number of urban planning experts and progressive thinkers have explored the concept of beauty enhancing the quality of life in the communities where people live and work. Gallup conducted the *Soul of the Community* survey and found that beauty enhances our sense of well-being and encourages our attachment to our community. In her book *On Beauty and Being Just*, Harvard philosopher Elaine Scarry asserts that beautiful natural surroundings tend to make people kinder, more interested in fairness, and more interested in stewardship, i.e., taking care of the community. "Mayor Smith loves our culture and history," Lynn Sordel said. "We've done a lot of tangible visual things to improve the aesthetics of the city."

The city has nine boards and commissions that work to advise the city council and the Mayor. Art Commissioner **Lynn Hanson,** owner of the Lynn Hanson Gallery, recently renewed her second term on the Art Commission. The commission was formed with the mission of furthering art in Lynnwood. The commission's projects include wrapping utility boxes. The wraps have different themes or campaigns, such as the welcoming message that was created to honor the Sister City relationship with Damyang Korea. Other campaigns include collaborations with Lynnwood schools and their students. Arts Commission projects include working with the new Community Justice Center that is currently in development.

"They have been asking the commission for ideas about what type of art to install," Hanson said. "We hope to have some input with the light rail station coming—the plan is they will have lightboxes to display art."

Prior to the pandemic, the Art Commission was integral to a large collaborative event that included art, food booths, wine tasting and musicians. Artists worked in booths during the event, where they showed their art.

"The event used to be held in February. It was canceled for 2020 and 2021 due to the pandemic," Hanson said. "Maybe in 2022, we can have the event again, and do something for the arts in Lynnwood."

Another way to instill a sense of community was by bringing people together. **Benjamin Goodwin** served on the city council from 2011 until 2019, and during the last three years, he served as president of the city council. Today he is an attorney with The Law Offices of Zachor and Thomas, Inc. Goodwin said, "Mayor Smith encouraged The Community Street Fair on 44th, known simply as *The Fair on 44th*. The fair was usually held the second week in September. Even the pandemic didn't stop the fair. In 2020, they had a drive-thru event.

The growing sense of community in Lynnwood is part of Mayor Smith's legacy. Lynn Hanson said, "Lynnwood is growing and feels like a welcoming place to live. I feel safe. It feels like a safe city, especially after working in Seattle's Pioneer Square. I see all of the new buildings coming in. I've been happy about all of the art being installed."

Soon a sculpture will be installed in front of the Lynnwood Convention Center. The sculpture of a giant neon heart spells out *Love Lynnwood* in letters. "When you're getting off the freeway you will see *Love Lynnwood* all lit up," Hanson said. The sculpture has been in the works for several years.

Nicola Smith has been described by many as a mayor with a heart. She remembered people's birthdays and she remembered their favorite candies. Sometimes people in public life maintain a public persona that is quite different from who they are in real life. Not so with the seventh mayor of Lynnwood. She has always been the same person onstage and off stage. As mayor, working with administrators, working with the council, or as a woman taking a walk on the beach with a dear friend, she was the same person—and that authenticity leads to integrity.

Senator Marko Liias said, "Nicola has had an incredible career in public service, and I will miss her gracious, steady hand. The next person will pick up the baton and lead forward. Regardless of who is the next mayor, Nicola is still a voice people will remember and listen to."

Benjamin Goodwin recalled the times she gave him handmade gifts—small gifts—a painted rock, the size of a silver dollar, hand-painted in an intricate design. "There was a message, generally about perseverance or understanding or healing. There were very tense times between the council and the administration, especially around budget time. Her goal was to help the city council understand where the administration was coming from in their decision and how the council would impact what they could or could not do."

Lynn Hanson remembers the mayor always showing up at the Arts Commission meetings and giving generously of her time. Hanson felt that if she ever had a concern, she would be able to get to the mayor and talk to her about it. Hanson said she once mentioned to the mayor that she was working on speaking in Danish. As it turned out Nicola speaks fluent Danish, so whenever Hanson saw her, she spoke to her in Danish. "She seems to always remember what people talked to her about. I wish she was running for mayor again. I'm going to miss her a lot."

Zabine Van Ness remembered when her husband died, the mayor was the first at her door with an armful of roses. "She is not a talker. She's a doer," Van Ness said. "You're either audacious and courageous or you're not."

For a mayor to be a genuine human being and a strong leader infused the entire city organization with efficiency, innovation and pride. Phong Nguyen remembers running into the mayor at the dollar store on I-99 on Valentine's Day. She was there to get a Valentine's Day card for Del. She was going to be in Olympia all day.

"After running into her in the dollar store. I was impressed that our mayor shops at the dollar store too. She's just like us. She's one of us."

Christine Frizzell said, "I've seen her at the senior center. I've seen her at the Mesika trail on cleanup day. She's the biggest ambassador for the city at the same time there is a level-headedness. She is genuinely interested in people."

Murals have appeared in the Lynnwood parks. At South Lynnwood Park, the artist Gabrielle Abbot created the *Grateful Steward* mural.5 The *Grateful Steward* design is inspired by the First Nations cultures and features animals and plants that were part of the daily lives of the First Nations people. The First Nations see themselves as stewards of the land, not owners of it. As our modern society grapples with the effects of climate change and globalization, we can all take guidance from the wisdom of the indigenous cultures whose territory we share. The mural will remind us that caring for the earth is a privilege and an honor, and so is caring for a community and all of its people.

Mayor Nicola Smith left the City of Lynnwood in a better place than she found it. The notion of stewardship comes to mind. A strong leader is a steward of the people. A steward feels gratitude for having had the opportunity to serve the people. In parting, the mayor has some advice to give to her successor:

---

[5] Portions of this project are made possible through the contributions of The Trust for Public Land and Kaiser Permanente, two Washington State Recreation & Conservation Office grants, and a Land and Water Conservation Fund grant.

You are a strong mayor, the CEO of the city's staff and the entire organization. Your focus needs to be on leading the city with a strong vision by having a clear plan. Build and nurture the plan to achieve a community vision. Empower your staff and set the expectation for excellence. Demand excellence from yourself and everyone around you. Demand continual improvements for efficiency and organizational excellence. Always ask: 'How can we do better?'

Most likely you do not have expertise in all of the areas that the city has to manage: engineering, sewer treatment, plant chemistry, parks development, ADA compliance, codes, permitting, financing, accounting, auditing, mechanics, economic development, policing, public relations, labor; therefore, one of your most important responsibilities will be to hire good people. Work closely with Human Resources to recruit, retain and develop the talent that best matches the jobs that are needed to run the city. Make sure that you hire staff who are intelligent, capable and who care about doing the best job possible for the people of Lynnwood.

Hold fast to your mission and vision by making certain all of the city's work is focused, determined and resilient. Always keep an eye on the ball. Clarity and transparency are crucial. Make certain every employee understands "why" his or her job is critical to the city's mission—which is to serve the people of Lynnwood.

Good communication is the most important tool you have. Provide open and safe paths of communication for employees and community members. Develop safe pathways for people to follow and trust your lead. Always keep your door open. Make every member of the community feel welcome.

Act as a connector between problems and solutions. Introduce people and organizations to each other. Making introductions gives people the opportunity to become stronger together. Never make promises until you have done your due diligence. Be curious and explore all angles, reimagine all possibilities.

As mayor, it is important for you to forge strong relationships between the Executive and Legislative branches of government. Build trust with the city council by giving them the best possible information so they can conduct timely and informed legal policymaking. Never lose sight of equity and justice and all of the ways you can serve the community by offering accessibility to the city's services and programs.

Love and honor the opportunity to be Mayor. It's kinda a big deal. Be aware that a good leader isn't liked by everyone. Don't take your critics personally. Be prepared to put on your Teflon shield and let the negative slide off. Be brave when sharing your "good ideas" and humble when accepting critical feedback. Be an inspiration, reliable and worthy of trust. Respect the "greater good" and always work toward collaboration. Celebrate success!

Thank you for the opportunity to serve you!
Warmly, Nicola

CHRONOLOGY OF EVENTS

November 5, 2013, Nicola Smith wins the mayoral race over incumbent Don Gough. Smith had 61.4%, or 2076 votes. Gough had 1,284 votes or just under 38%.

December 2013, Mayor-elect Nicola Smith travels to Haiti.

Monday, December 9, 2013, Nicola Smith is sworn in as the seventh Mayor of Lynnwood by Municipal Court Judge Stephen Moore.

June 11, 2014, Mayor Smith delivers her first State of the City Address at the Lynnwood Convention Center.

August 28, 2015, Mayor Smith hosts the first Veterans Roundtable aimed at creating a Veteran-Supportive City.

September 22, 2016, Sister City Signing Ceremony and Reception to celebrate the formation of the Sister City relationship with Damyang, South Korea.

November 8, 2016, Sound Transit 3 **was** approved by over 54% of voters in the Puget Sound region; voters in Pierce County rejected the measure, but the measure **passed** in King and Snohomish counties and had an overall majority.

January 23, 2017, city council adopted Ordinance 3247 authorizing the creation of the new Diversity, Equity & Inclusion Commission (DEI)

January 23, 2017, Resolution 2017-03 adopted confirming Lynnwood's commitment to being a safe, welcoming, and equitable community for all.

January 31, 2017, Grand Opening of the Heroes' Café at Verdant Wellness Center

May 6, 2017, Grand Opening of the Northwest Veterans Heritage Museum at Heritage Park

August 1, 2017, Proposition 1 approved the creation of the South Snohomish County Fire & Rescue Regional Fire Authority (54.4% yes / 45.6% no)

Sunday, October 1, 2017, South Snohomish County Fire and Rescue officially formed

November 7, 2017, Mayor Nicola Smith Wins Reelection against Council Member George Hurst (56.72% / 43.16%)

March 2019, the City of Lynnwood joins the Government Alliance for Racial Equity and Mayor Smith assembles a cross-departmental team of 12 employees to join the learning cohort.

June 2019, Mayor Smith along with Public Works Director, City Engineer, and Federal Lobbyist advocate for Federal Transportation Funds in Washington D.C.

January 16, 2020, Mayor Nicola Smith appointed to the board of Community Transit

February 19, 2020, Mayor Nicola Smith appointed to the board of Sound Transit

March 4, 2020, Mayor Smith declares a public emergency in the City of Lynnwood and begins our COVID-19 Pandemic Response.

September 21, 2020, Friendship City relationship with **Chilpancingo, Mexico** confirmed

December 14, 2020, Development and Business Services Department created, and David Kleitsch named first DBS Director.

January 24, 2021, Friendship City relationship with Bole Kefle Ketema, Wereda 10, Addis Ababa, Ethiopia confirmed.

INDEX

M

N

About Patricia Vaccarino

Patricia Vaccarino is an American writer. She has written award-winning film scripts, press materials, content, books, essays and articles. She has published four novels, and four nonfiction books. She founded the P.R. firm Xanthus Communications LLC, and the internet media company, PR for People®, where people share their news. She has an audience of 40,000+ followers on social media. She divides her time between homes in downtown Seattle and the north coast of Oregon.

www.ingramcontent.com/pod-product-compliance
Lightning Source LLC
Chambersburg PA
CBHW072046080426
42733CB00010B/2011